VOICES FROM THE STORY

VOICES FROM THE STORY

By

Rev. Dr. Sally Stevens Smith

Order this book online at www.trafford.com
or email orders@trafford.com

Most Trafford titles are also available at major online book retailers.

Printed in the United States of America.

ISBN: 978-1-4269-6014-7 (sc)
ISBN: 978-1-4269-6016-1 (e)

Library of Congress Control Number: 2011903904

Trafford rev. 04/08/2011

 www.trafford.com

North America & International
toll-free: 1 888 232 4444 (USA & Canada)
phone: 250 383 6864 ♦ fax: 812 355 4082

For Walter,

master preacher and storyteller,

with love and gratitude

"When I was a child, I read these
Biblical tales with a wonder mixed with anguish.
I imagined Isaac on the altar and I cried.
I saw Joseph, prince of Egypt, and I laughed.
Why dwell on them again? And why now?
It falls to the story teller to explain."

Elie Wiesel, in *Messengers of God*

TABLE OF CONTENTS

Old Testament Voices

New Testament Voices

PREFACE

THE STORY

Christians exist as people of a story. We find that story in the Bible, and call it The Story because we believe it is nothing less than the story of God's saving work in history.

In the Hebrew Scriptures, the Old Testament, The Story begins with prehistory. God creates a good world filled with creatures that live in peace, and crowns creation with the human beings who are called to care for all the rest. Even though they dwell in an earthly garden paradise, those first humans find it impossible to obey God, opening the way for sin and evil. God evicts them from paradise and they go out to live in a fallen world. God could have abandoned them to their own devices, but instead starts the process of reconciliation and healing called salvation.

The narrative continues with the astounding affirmation that God, Yahweh, Creator of the heavens and earth, chooses to enter into covenant with one people who will be instruments of salvation. God enters into this relationship, not with a mighty nation, but with Israel, also called the Hebrews or Jews, a powerless and politically insignificant people.

God calls Abraham and Sarah to move from their home in Haran to a new land and found a great nation "in whom all the families of the earth shall be blessed." (Genesis 12:3) Yahweh gives them this assignment despite the fact that the couple is elderly and has no children. In faith, Abraham and Sarah go out, not knowing where they are to go. After years of waiting, doubting and trusting, Sarah gives birth to Isaac, who becomes the father of Jacob and Esau.

Jacob and his wives have twelve sons, each of whom represents one of the tribes of Israel. Joseph, one of Jacob's sons, goes to Egypt as a slave, but becomes Pharaoh's right hand man. A great famine ensues and the Hebrews to go down to Egypt to find food. They settle there, only to be enslaved when a new Pharaoh comes to power. Yahweh hears their cries, and calls Moses to confront Pharaoh and command him to "Let my people go." Finally, Pharaoh agrees to free the Israelites and they make their exodus from Egypt, narrowly escaping across the Sea of Reeds. They understand their liberation as God's direct saving action in history, and The Exodus, becomes the defining story of their faith and life.

The scriptures go on to tell of how Yahweh leads the people through the wilderness, creates covenant with them and gives them *Torah*, the law, to live by. But the people are faithless, and God waits until a generation is gone, before bringing them into Canaan, the Promised Land.

From there, The Story describes the people's struggle to know the meaning of chosen-ness, its gifts and responsibilities. It presents the drama of how God continues to love and care for the people despite their constant faithlessness and apostasy. Despite the warnings of the prophets, the people are finally judged, punished and sent into exile. Even in those terrible experiences, the Hebrews know Yahweh as their God, and themselves as Yahweh's people.

After many years, God brings the Hebrews home and they rebuild. Eager to protect their heritage and traditions, many become ingrown and narrow in their thinking. Rigidity in interpreting the law and suspicion of non-Jews are common. Into this milieu, Jesus of Nazareth is born.

In the Christian scriptures, the New Testament, the story affirms that God's very self enters human life in Jesus of Nazareth. As the living expression of God's love, Jesus, the Christ or Messiah, shares our common lot. He is Emmanuel, God with us, the fulfillment of God's saving purpose. He gathers disciples who join him in the work of proclaiming God's rule and spreading God's seeking and inclusive love. The world rejects that kind of love and puts Jesus to death on a cross.

Jesus' death is not the end of The Story. God raises him from the dead, winning the decisive battle over sin and death. Great pain and struggle remain in this world, but Easter is the assurance that God will win the final victory. The story of Jesus' life, passion and resurrection defines our existence as Christians, just as the exodus does for the Jews.

Fifty days after the resurrection, on the Jewish festival of Pentecost, God's Holy Spirit arrives in wind and fire. The Spirit gathers Jesus' disciples as the church and sends them out to witness to the good news of God's saving love. As the covenant community grows, it expands to include, not only Jews, but Gentiles and all who respond to the Christ in faith and commit their lives to God through him.

The Story is one great narrative, but it is made up of many stories. The primary Character throughout is God, but the many other characters bring to life the way God works with the world and people. Based on the biblical texts, supplemented by historical background and imagination, this collection of first person story/sermons seeks to present the experiences of some of these characters and the action of God in their lives.

Each story/sermon offers a message for the present as well. When we cross over into the lives of the ancient biblical people, we discover insights and challenges that can build and strengthen our faith. We see how these people deal with joy and sorrow, loss and fear, conflict, relationships and other issues. Like them, we can discover and embrace God's faithful care and learn to trust more fully. In some cases, the message or insight of the story is intrinsic within it. In others, I add reflections which relate the character's experience to our own.

My hope is that as you read, your will hear what these voices from The Story are saying to your life.

The Rev. Dr. Sally Stevens Smith

ACKNOWLEDGMENTS

I am grateful to the congregations of Union Congregational Church, UCC, Angels Camp, California, and Jamestown United Methodist Church, Jamestown, California, and to my friends Reuel Nash and Carol Churchill for listening and encouraging me to collect and share these first person story/sermons.

Many thanks also to INKLINGS, my writing group, for critiquing many of the story/sermons; and to my sister, Phyllis Endicott and friends Chuck and Camilla Peterson and Vicky Oneto for reviewing the text.

The enthusiasm and support of my family and other friends is deeply appreciated as well.

OLD TESTAMENT
VOICES

1

MARKED

(Based on Genesis 4:1-16)

This morning I invite you to move back with me time out of mind, to the days before history began.

Travel back to a time that is not limited to one place and time, but which touches all places and all times.

Move backward with me and quietly slip yourself into the skin of the man called Cain, son of Adam and Eve.

Be Cain. Experience the world from inside his head, his heart, his whole being.

Hear him speak.

* * * * *

Listen. I have a story to tell you. You think you've seen hard times? Just wait until you hear what happened to me. It's the worst deal I've ever heard of.

My name is Cain. I'm the eldest son of Adam and Eve. You've heard of them haven't you—the first man and woman who lived in a beautiful garden called Eden?

Well, they were my first problem. Our God, Yahweh, put them in that garden to take care of the rest of creation. It was a great place to live, like a park, with plenty of water and all kinds of trees and flowers. There were all kinds of animals too, but they lived together in peace.

All my parents had to do was enjoy everything and do a little gardening. You know—keep the weeds down, prune, break off dead blooms—no real heavy work. Here there were no pests to worry about, everything just grew as it should. What a life!

But then they blew it. Besides caring for the garden, the only thing God asked them to do was to stay away from one particular tree, the tree of the knowledge of good and evil. Could they do that one little thing? No.

Of course they said it wasn't their fault. Dad blamed it on Mom, because she offered him a piece of fruit from the forbidden tree. He even blamed God for making Mom. And Mom—she couldn't own up either. She passed the buck to some smart talking snake who told her to pick the fruit. The snake didn't say a thing.

Yahweh God was so mad! They had the whole garden, why couldn't they do just one thing in return? For punishment they got kicked out of that wonderful place, and went to live east of Eden, away from all its beauty and peace. They always talked about it, but how I wish I had seen it for myself.

Well, let me go on. There they were out in the cold, cruel world, the world where I was born. Abel was there too—he's my younger brother. You can imagine the boring time I had growing up—only parents and one brother around. No other kids to play with, no girls. It was a real drag. I knew it would have been different if we could have stayed in that garden.

When I grew old enough to think about a job, I decided that what I really wanted to do with my life was to create another wonderful garden. I knew it wouldn't be as good as Eden, God's garden, but it would be very good. I love the soil and trees and flowers and plants, and decided that a farmer's life was the life for me. It was no small thing either, I was going to invent what you now call agriculture. I tried to talk Abel into joining me, but he was the restless type, and more into animals than plant life. He liked tending his sheep and roaming around the hills with them. As soon as he could he went off to get his own flock and become a shepherd. To each his own.

I worked hard on my farming. It wasn't easy. I found a spot near the river with lush and fertile soil and started cultivating. My grapevines grew thick and strong and their grapes were the best. What flavor they had! Other fruits and nuts began to bear. I loved the olives and figs. There were more than enough and I was very thankful. I decided to prepare a fine offering for Yahweh, our God.

About that time, Abel came by to say hello. We sat down to talk and he told me he was preparing an offering too. He was planning to sacrifice one of his best lambs. We decided to go and make our offerings together.

The next day was bright and cloudless. I thought of the good soil Yahweh had given me, the seed and the sun and the water. Lovingly, I prepared a basket of my most luscious fruit: pomegranates bursting with juice, clusters of grapes, delicious dates and figs. Then I added some of my best nuts and prize vegetables. I stood back and admired the basket. It was a handsome thank offering and I was eager to offer it to the Lord.

Abel and I set out for the offering place—he with his fine lamb and me with my overflowing basket. It was a pleasure to walk out on such a lovely morning. We had a good talk too. Now that we were both doing well in work we love we seemed to get along better than ever.

We arrived at our destination and set down our gifts on the simple altar. Then we knelt and prayed. When we rose up and looked at the offerings to see if Yahweh was pleased, I stepped back in shock. Yahweh had refused my sacrifice and accepted Abel's. Now Abel's lamb was good and all, but so was my beautiful produce. Why didn't God accept both?

At first I just stood there, stunned, but then I felt anger creeping into me, running hot through my veins. I could feel my skin flushing, my face falling, my fists clenching. I felt no good, rejected. Inside I heard myself shouting, "Why? Why? WHY? Why don't you accept my gift? Why Abel's and not mine? What a miserably unfair God you are, Yahweh!"

Yahweh could see my anger and spoke to me. "Cain, why are you angry? Why has your face fallen? If you do well, won't you be accepted? And if you do not do well, sin is lurking at the door like a wild beast. Its desire is for you but you may choose to master it."

Burning with anger, I thought, but didn't dare say, "What in the world is all that about? I have done well, very well. I brought my best offering and you turned it down. What do you want of me anyway?"

Some people say that you have to be a shepherd or wandering herder to get in good with God--not one of us more settled types. Maybe they're right, but why? It's not fair, not fair at all! Both kinds of work need doing in this world. If Yahweh prefers lamb chops to ripe pomegranates and figs, OK. But isn't it possible to be polite about it? I remember last year when I was longing for a new plough and my dad gave me a ewe lamb. I didn't want that lamb or need her either. Dad always gave me what Abel wanted—he never seemed to understand what I wanted—but did I say, "Keep your old lamb"? No. I said, "Thank you" with a smile, and took good care of her.

Even if my gift wasn't up to par, you'd think God would be kind enough to soften the blow. But no, all Yahweh did was give me advice. "Chill! Calm down and be careful." Just remembering makes me tremble with anger. A God who can't even be polite, who is less kind than I am! Who is this Yahweh anyway!

You have probably heard the rest of my story. It's not easy to talk about. The anger I felt toward God that day kept growing into a cold hard, relentless fury. Maybe it was because I didn't know how to deal with God, but somehow it seemed that the whole thing was Abel's fault. He'd weaseled in and taken all of Yahweh's approval for himself. And suddenly I hated Abel, my own brother.

Then came that fateful day. I planned it to the last detail. I invited Abel to go for a walk into a field, out of earshot and out of sight of others. Then, while Abel was chattering on about how many new lambs were due this spring, I grasped the heavy wooden staff I was carrying by my side and swung it hard. My first blow knocked Abel down and stunned him. Then I rose up and swung again, hitting him squarely on the head. I killed him. I killed him dead.

Quickly, I knelt down and heaped soft earth around him. When he was fully covered I prepared to go back home. As I trudged along, feelings of remorse began to creep into my mind and heart. Had I actually killed my brother?

Then I heard a voice calling to me. Had someone seen me kill Abel after all? I looked all around but didn't see a soul. The voice called again. "Cain, Cain, where is your brother?" It was a strong voice, but it sounded infinitely sad. I realized it was Yahweh.

I walked on, pretending not to hear. "Your brother, Cain, where is your brother?"

Deciding to brazen it out, I answered, "How should I know? He's not my problem. Am I my brother's keeper?"

But I couldn't fool Yahweh—Yahweh knows everything. And all of us Hebrews know that the life of a person is in the blood and my brother's blood was calling out from the ground. His blood had summoned the Lord of life.

I braced myself for punishment. When it came, it was worse than I could ever have imagined. God said, "When you till the ground, the earth will no longer yield its strength to you; and you will be a fugitive and wanderer on the earth." Can you imagine? Here I am a farmer, I don't know how to do anything else. I love a settled life, close to the earth, but now I must wander instead.

I cried out to Yahweh, "My punishment is more than I can bear. Today you are driving me away from the soil. I will be hidden from you, a fugitive and wanderer upon the earth, and anyone who wants to can kill me."

But then God said, "No. Whoever kills you will suffer sevenfold vengeance." Then Yahweh put a mark on me, so that no one would dare to kill me, and sent me away....

So now I ask you again, who can say that life is good? It seems like the cards were stacked against me from the beginning. Think about it:

Before I am even born, my parents get kicked out of our home because they couldn't resist temptation. Why didn't God make them obedient instead of giving them free will? Poor planning!

Then, they work hard and I do too, making the best of a bad deal. I offer God my finest produce only to have it turned down—FOR NO REASON!

The anger God gave me—yes God created my emotions—grows unmanageable and I kill my brother, the brother I love.

It was a set up. I didn't want to kill Abel, but how could I stand it—being rejected while he was reveling in God's approval.

So now I'm being sent off, away from all I know and love. And it's all because of an unfair, capricious God who plays favorites.

It's a raw deal. Don't tell me that God is good, life is good!

* * * * *

Now, let's come back to the present, to our own lives. How do you feel about life? Does it seem pretty good to you? Or do you agree with Cain?

Do you ever agonize over the unfairness we see and experience from childhood on? As infants, eagerly exploring, we reach out to touch, only to have our hand slapped. "Don't knock over that china vase." "Keep away from that hot stove." Our questing is thwarted and we must capitulate. The world is not "ours" after all, and it doesn't seem fair.

And unfairness is part and parcel of the wider world. Think of the problem of hunger. Why do millions of people go hungry every day? Why isn't there a meal for every mouth? Why are so few of us consuming so much? Why do some have enough while others starve? There is no moral reason for the inequity—it just isn't fair. And hunger is only one of the ills of our planet—only one of the injustices we see and hear of every day.

Let's look again at the story of Cain, his experience of rejection. I don't pretend to have an explanation for the mystery of God's behavior in the story, but can you just accept it without question? Does something inside you cry out in protest? It does in me. How can our loving God be so unreasonably unfair? I feel with Cain, and hurt with him.

Author John Steinbeck felt it too. He based one of his greatest novels, *East of Eden,* on the story of Cain and Abel. In it he demonstrates the effects of acceptance and rejection between fathers and sons, brother and brother. In the story, the father Adam Trask, was himself a favored son, and continues the pattern of favoritism with his twin sons Caleb and Aaron. Cal is tempted toward evil because of his persistent inability to please his father.

In the novel, Lee, the wise Chinese houseman, reminds Caleb of the teaching in the biblical story of Cain. Cal does not have to give in to the sin that is crouching at the door, ready to overwhelm him. He is free to choose life and overcome it. But like Cain, Cal can't say no to his anger. He succumbs to its power and tragedy ensues. And yet, at the end of the novel, Cal's father finally blesses him, reminding Cal that he may still choose to live well.

Maybe you have experienced rejection at home or school or work. Do you remember having everyone chosen for the team except you, or trying to share an important experience with your spouse, who is too busy watching the game to listen? And some rejections are far worse—being abandoned by a person you love, or rejecting yourself as no good. Rejection is a terrible, anger producing reality. It can create a desire to strike out, get revenge.

Cain acted out his anger in murder, an utterly unacceptable act. We need to learn how to deal with rejection and anger without turning to violence. We must find ways to work through our anger and turn life's garbage into flowers.

Cain's question still sounds. In a world like ours do we dare to say that life is good? I believe we can. Think back to the end of Cain's story. When Cain cries out that his punishment is more than he can bear, that he will be prey for anyone, Yahweh says, "Not so," and marks him with a particular mark. Many people think that the mark proclaimed Cain a murderer, but that was not its meaning or purpose. If you look at the Genesis text carefully, it is clear that the mark is a sign of God's protection. No one may kill Cain. Like all life, Cain belongs to God.

So ultimately, the end of Cain's story is not rejection, but grace, and so is the end of ours. If you ever feel like Cain—a rejected wanderer—even at those times you can know yourself as belonging to God. The bottom line of life is that God loves us, and does not forsake us, even at our worst.

As Christians we dare to say even more. In the end, we are not rejected, but accepted. We worship the One who came not for the righteous, but sinners, the One who came to seek and to save the lost. Because of Jesus, who shared our common lot, our human joys, trials and struggles, we have a model for true living, and a source of the power we need to cope with unfairness and rejection. We can decide to stop wandering and follow him faithfully on the pathway toward love and reconciliation, justice and peace. May it be so.

2

GOD MAKES LAUGHTER

(Based on Genesis 12, 16, 18:1-15, 21:1-7 and Hebrews 11:1-3, 8, 11-12)

I am hobbling around the kitchen getting supper, sitting down now and then to save my bad knee, when Abraham, my dear old husband, bursts into the room.

"Start packing, Sarah, we're moving."

"Moving" I cry. "Why? Where? I don't want to move, I like it here."

I am confused and upset. Here we are—comfortably settled in Haran, with a well organized household and many animals. A move seems disruptive and unnecessary. My wonder only increases as Abraham explains why we're going. "Yahweh, our God, spoke to me and told me we must go."

"Well then, where?"

"I don't know yet, Sarah, but don't worry. God will show us."

"Hmm," I mumble skeptically.

"But listen, says Abraham, "That's not all. Wait till you hear the promise. Yahweh is planning to show us a new land and make us into a great nation. God will bless us, and make us a blessing to all the families of the earth."

"Husband," I say, trying to be reasonable in the face of this unreasonable vision, "we do not have even one child, how can we found a whole nation?"

"Have faith, Sarah. Trust Yahweh."

"Have faith, Sarah. Trust Yahweh"—that's the story of my life. It's been my story since that first time I heard about God calling Abraham, and it continues through all our ups and downs. Needless to say, we do pack up and leave Haran without any idea of where we're going. What a job it is loading up our household goods, and then marching off in a caravan with all our people, camels and other animals!

I'm not young, but I'm still pretty good looking if I do say so myself, and when we stop in Egypt on the way Abraham grows afraid. He thinks the Pharaoh will kill him and take me as a concubine if he says that I'm his wife. So what does my dear husband do but say I'm his sister? That doesn't sound like being faithful to the promise to me, and apparently it doesn't to God either. Yahweh gets really angry, and sends a plague on the Pharaoh. Then the Pharaoh gets mad at Abraham for his lie, but luckily he doesn't kill him. He just gives me back to my husband, and we go on our way.

When we get re-settled—O yes, our destination turns out to be a place called Canaan—Abraham keeps talking about the promise, the promise, the promise. One day, Yahweh appears to him and they make a covenant agreement. Abraham is all excited about it, but it sounds fantastic to me. In their covenant, Abraham vows to obey Yahweh, and Yahweh promises to give us descendants as numerous as the stars in the heavens so we can found that nation we keep hearing about. This, even though we still don't have one child to our name, let alone the son of the promise.

At this point I start thinking seriously about the child we're supposed to have in our old age. This trust business is all very well, but maybe the only way is for me to make it happen. Among our people, if you have a maidservant, custom allows her bear a child for her mistress. The servant becomes a surrogate mother. Your husband lies with her. When she gets pregnant, she carries the baby and bears it, but the child belongs to you as the mistress of the house. So one evening I talk with Abraham about the idea, and he agrees to do whatever I want. Just maybe, this plan will make God's promise a reality.

After thinking about it a long time I tell Abraham, "Let's go ahead." He takes my Egyptian maid, Hagar, to his bed, and before long she is with child. It makes me sick with jealousy, but after all it is for Abraham and me, and may solve the problem of our future.

It is good to think that I will actually have a child to call my own, but the way Hagar treats me is anything but good. Instead of returning to her role as an obedient servant, the minute she gets pregnant she flounces around as if she were the lady of the house instead of me. She treats me with contempt, giving me sly looks and acting as if she is superior because she's going to bear Abraham's child. Unbelievable!

I complain to Abraham, and he just says, "Well, she's your servant, you can do whatever you want with her." So I do. I clamp down on Hagar's behavior, and treat her harshly. Before I know it, she runs away, and I find myself with mixed feelings. I want that child she's carrying, but not her high and mighty presence.

After a few days she comes back, dirty and bedraggled and hanging her head as she stands before me. "Mistress Sarah," she says, "When I was thirsty in the wilderness, God gave me water, and told me to come back and submit to you, so here I am." After insisting on a lot of assurances about her behavior, I agree to take her back. After all, she is carrying Abraham's child, and her attitude toward me is improved. A few weeks later, Hagar bears a son to Abraham and names him Ishmael.

Not long after this, Yahweh God comes to Abraham again, and repeats the promise. Abraham asks God to accept Ishmael as the child of the promise, but Yahweh says, "No. I will bless Ishmael, but Sarah is the one who will bear the son of promise and become the mother of nations."

Then, even Abraham, who never seems to question God the way I do, has to laugh. When he comes home he tells me "Sarah, I laughed so hard I rolled on the ground. I just couldn't help it. But Yahweh keeps on insisting that we're going to have our own child, and that his name will be Isaac, which means, 'he laughs.'"

"We'll see," I think with a sigh.

One day the next summer, Abraham is relaxing outside the tent under the shade of our oak trees when three strange men approach. I peer out of the tent, wondering who these visitors might be and where they are from. They're on foot, they have no pack animals, and they aren't even carrying water in this desert heat. Abraham jumps up and approaches the men, "Welcome, welcome. Please don't pass us by. Won't you sit down and rest, and let us wash the dust from off your feet. Have some water and bread to refresh you." Abraham is always hospitable, but he seems to realize these guests are unusual and deserve our very best.

They sit down and Abraham rushes into the tent saying," Sarah, take some flour and make cakes right away." Then he calls a servant, "Hurry. Prepare a calf for our guests to enjoy." When the food is all ready he takes out curds and milk too, and stands beside the men while they eat."

I stay standing near the entrance to the tent so I can hear them talking. When they are finished eating, the men thank Abraham and one asks him, "Where is your wife, Sarah." All of a sudden, I realize it is none less than Yahweh, the Lord, who is speaking.

"Sarah is in the tent," says Abraham.

The Lord continues. "In the springtime I will surely return and Sarah will bear you a son."

"Here we go again with that ridiculous promise," Laughing quietly to myself, I think, "I don't even bleed any more. How can I possibly have a child?"

Then the Lord says to Abraham, "Why did Sarah laugh? Is anything too hard for the Lord?'

"Oh no, God heard me." I am afraid and come out of the tent. I speak up, "Sir, I did not laugh."

But God says, "No, you did laugh."

After that day, I wonder if I have ruined everything. Will God hold my laughter against us? But no, wonder of wonders, the following spring I find I am indeed with child. No expectant mother ever had better care. Abraham treats me with extraordinary tenderness, as if I were some sort of fragile doll. He makes the servants wait on me hand and foot and I reach my lying-in rested and healthy.

Finally the moment comes and Isaac is born whole and strong—child of the promise. They say that babies don't smile from the beginning, but he looks as if he is grinning at us, ready to burst into a big laugh and say, "See, I'm here, no matter what you thought."

Abraham and I gaze at him with love and joy. I say "God has made laughter for me!" Then we both burst out laughing!

Why am I telling you this strange story—so long ago and far away? I am telling you because I hope you will dare to trust God to do good things, even to make laughter, in your life.

You may be having a hard time. You may be finding it difficult to smile, let alone laugh. But from the beginning God has made and kept promises to person after person. Sometimes it seems that they cannot possibly come true. But when you feel discouraged, remember my story, and the child who finally was born as the first of a great nation. Dare to trust that God loves you too, and is working to create goodness in your life.

Your life may not turn out the way you hope. You may not find the health or relationships or achievement you long for. It is possible, that there will be many problems, obstacles and hard jolts along your way. But I believe that if you can trust in God's great faithfulness, and believe that God is walking beside you, you will find peace in your journey, your will find courage in your journey, and you will arrive at a destination that is right for you. May it be so.

3

GRACE IN THE DESERT

(Based on Genesis 16, 21:1-21 and 25:12-18)

The sand dunes seem to go on forever here in the wilderness of Beer-Sheba. They are dotted with scrubby bushes here and there, but they offer no shade to speak of. We've been wandering for two days and I have no idea where we are. Clutching little Ishmael by the hand, half carrying him, I stagger on. My strength is fading fast in this relentless sun and his is already gone. Finally we come to a slightly bigger bush, with a few leaves clinging to its branches. Tenderly, I settle my little son in its sparse shade and collapse beside him.

He asks hopefully, "Mother, may I have a drink?" I take the skin of water from my shoulder and shake it. Perhaps there are a few drops left.

Here you are, my son." I give him the skin and he lifts it to his lips, moistening them with our last bit of water.

"Is there any more?"

"No, my dear, and our bread is gone too. Just try to lie back and rest."

Ishmael lies down on the sand and tries to get comfortable. I sit beside him, thinking of how our lives have come to this pass.

I was only a young girl, growing up poor in Egypt, when a rich Hebrew named Abraham bought me as a slave. He said, "I want you to have a good Hebrew name, so I will call you Hagar." Then he took me away from my family and the only life I knew, all the way to Haran, in Palestine.

When we arrived, Abraham gave me to his wife, Sarah, as a maidservant. Both he and Sarah were kind, and for some time my life went along smoothly. I loved brushing Sarah's long shiny black hair, and keeping her pretty clothing in good repair.

Abraham and Sarah seemed to have everything, but she often talked about the great heartache of their lives, the lack of a child. Besides, their God, Yahweh, had promised Abraham that they would have a son who was chosen to be the first of many descendants, a whole new nation. They have tried to hold on to faith in the promise, but it was taking so long and they were growing old.

Then one day, Sarah called me to her and told me their amazing plan. The Hebrews have a custom of having a maidservant bear a child for her mistress. It sounded strange to me, but this is what happens. The master takes the maid to his bed, and when she becomes pregnant, she carries the child and gives birth, but the child belongs not to her, but to her mistress.

I wasn't given any choice in the matter. Abraham and Sarah had decided that using me as a surrogate mother might be their only chance to have a child. So I went to Abraham's bed when they told me to. When I started being sick in the morning, I realized that I was indeed pregnant.

They were happy, and so was I, but before long my good relationship with Sarah changed. She said that I was treating her with contempt because I was pregnant and she was not, and grew very angry. I tried not to be arrogant, but I admit that I was proud of carrying Abraham's child. It was hard not to compare my fertility with Sarah's apparent barrenness.

Sarah went and complained to Abraham, and he said, "The girl belongs to you, Sarah, do with her as you wish." Then Sarah treated me harshly, giving me the hardest work to do, punishing me at the least provocation, even slapping me. I couldn't take it, and fled out to the wilderness of Shur, hoping that I might find my way back to Egypt.

That was my first taste of this barren wilderness and its privation. I was feeling lost and tired and very thirsty when I finally came to a spring and sank down beside it, closing my eyes. After awhile I heard a voice saying, "Hagar, maid of Sarah, where have you come from and where are you going?" It was the voice of their God, Yahweh.

"I am fleeing from my mistress, Sarah," I answered.

"Return to your mistress and submit to her, for you are going to bear a son, and have many descendants, because the Lord has heard your affliction. You shall call his name Ishmael; he will be fierce, a wild ass of a man, who will dwell over against all his kinsmen"

I was astounded that the Hebrew God would care about me, let alone appear to me, and said, "Thou art a God of seeing. Have I really seen God and lived?"

So I returned and hung my head before Sarah, "Please let me be your obedient servant once again." Her anger seemed spent, and she took me back. Of course, Abraham was glad to see me because the child I was carrying was his. When my time came, I bore my son, and Abraham called him Ishmael. God said he would be blessed, but that he was not the child of promise.

Ishmael was growing and thriving a few years later when Sarah announced that she actually was pregnant. The household could scarcely believe it, and after such a long wait, neither could Abraham and Sarah. Despite God's promise that they would have their own child, it had been hard for them to hang on to faith and hope.

Oh how carefully Sarah kept herself, and how tenderly Abraham and the whole household watched over her! At last Isaac was born, strong and healthy. His name means laughter, and he was indeed a happy baby, laughing all the time. At first everything went along fine, but one day when Sarah was watching Ishmael and Isaac playing together her gaze went dark, and she turned with a scowl on her face and went into the house to speak to Abraham.

I didn't know what she was saying to him, but before long Abraham came out wearing a long face. "Hagar, I don't know how to tell you this, but Sarah says I must cast you and Ishmael out of our household. She refuses to have Ishmael be an heir along with Isaac, or even to let them to play together. I don't want you to go, but God says I should do whatever Sarah says, since our descendants will be named through Isaac. I'm so sorry."

I froze, and stood there stunned, as he continued. "Go now. Get the boy and gather your things to leave early tomorrow. I will bring you some bread and water to take with you."

In the morning Ishmael and I got up early and tried to eat. Then we went outside, and there was Abraham, carrying a pouch of bread and a large skin of water that he slung over my shoulder. "Goodbye and go with God," he said as we turned away toward the looming wilderness.

Now it is two days later and the bread and water are gone. We are at the end of our strength. I cannot stand to sit here and watch Ishmael fail. I know he is dying. I shift his small body as far as possible under the shade of the bush, and move away off, the distance of a bowshot.

Then I hear Ishmael's little voice sobbing. Yahweh God hears too and calls to me. "Hagar, what is troubling you? Fear not, for I have heard the lad weeping. Arise, and lift him, take him by the hand, for I have plans for him. I will make him a great nation."

I jump up, eager to obey this voice of hope and salvation. Reaching under the bush I gently lift up my little boy. He opens his eyes and smiles weakly at me as I take his hand. Then my eyes are opened and I see a well of water. "Come, Ishmael, let me give you a drink." He drinks thirstily and I do too.

Soon after the water revives us, we find our way through the wilderness. Ishmael grows up loving the desert and settles down in the wilderness of Paran. He becomes a fine archer, and marries an Egyptian woman I find for him. And I? I become the grandmother of twelve tribal princes.

Looking back on that terrible time in the desert when I thought both Ishmael and I would die, I always remember how Abraham told me that God wanted the nation he and Sarah founded through Isaac to be a blessing to all nations. It doesn't matter if you are Jewish or Gentile or Arab, like us. God created, loves and cares for all people—the whole wide world. No exceptions!

From that day on we have known and trusted that no matter what happens, no matter how dark life looks, God is with us all today, and every day. We found grace in the desert and you can too.

4

THE DREAMER

(Based on Genesis 37-46 and 50)

INTRODUCTION

This story sermon is based on the saga of Joseph, the dreamer, and told in his voice.

It is one of the great narratives of the Old Testament—complete with a father who plays favorites, ten jealous brothers, and a cocky young hero of amazing talent and ability who grows into a brilliant, wise and forgiving leader.

Starting in chapter 37, the story takes up a big hunk of the book of Genesis. For the scripture, I suggest reading a brief section of the last chapter, where Joseph forgives his brothers yet again, and affirms his faith in God's providential work. Chapter 50:15-21

THE DREAMER

It is a sweltering trip out to the place where my brothers are keeping our sheep, but my father wants me to go and check on how they are doing. I'm almost there when I hear a shout, "Look. There he is, Joseph the dreamer."

Then Judah's voice. "This is our chance. Let's go get him and kill him. Let's rid ourselves of those insulting dreams once and for all."

More voices join in, "Yes! Let's get him." What can I do to protect myself out here so far from home? I know I annoy my brothers. They don't like me being our father's favorite and hearing about my dreams of glory, even though they're real. But I never realized they hate me enough to want to kill me.

Reuben responds. "No, no. We can't kill him. He is our brother and his blood would cry out from the ground. Just throw him into that deep pit over there." Can it be that Reuben is planning to try to rescue me later and take me home?

My brothers rush me; ripping off the beautiful long-sleeved coat of many colors my father has just given me. Then they grab me by both arms and drag me over to the pit. It is empty, deep and dry, with nary a drop of water or patch of shade, a terrifying place. They throw me in, and from the bottom I can see their shadows disappearing as they walk away and leave me.

It is totally silent. Probably they have gone over to the shady oasis to eat their lunch. After awhile, I hear the noise of men and animals, and soon my brothers are drawing me up out of the pit. At first I am relieved, but then I see a large caravan of Arab traders which has paused to get water. I don't see Reuben, and Judah seems to be in charge. He is dickering with the Arabs. Then one of them gives Judah some shekels, and strides over to where I am standing. He grabs me by the arm, ties a rope around my neck and leads me over to the caravan. "You're on your way to Egypt, my lad," he says, "you'll make a good strong slave."

As we move off, I turn back to see my brothers. They are looking after me with triumphant expressions on their faces. What will my father think when I don't come home? What will he do?

Well, I am not to know the answer to those questions for a long, long time. In the meantime I have to concentrate on survival. At least the traders give me food and water. They want me to stay strong so that I will bring a good price when they sell me.

In Egypt, they do get the price they want, and I am sent to the house of Potiphar, captain of the Pharaoh's guard. I am set to work inside as a house slave. I had rarely done much work at home, but it isn't hard to learn. I feel the presence of the Lord with me, and do my job well.

Potiphar notices me, and the skills I've developed. Then one day he stops me saying, "Joseph, I want you to be my personal servant." Not long after that he makes me his overseer, in charge of his house and everything he has. Now the only thing Potiphar has to think about for himself is what to choose for dinner.

Everything goes well, until Potiphar's wife starts complimenting me on my appearance, "You are so good looking—you'd never know that you're a slave." She gives me sultry looks and brushes against me whenever we pass one another. What is she up to?

It isn't long before I find out. One day, when Potiphar is out, she comes close to me and whispers "Lie with me."

"O, I cannot. Potiphar trusts me and has given his household into my care. I cannot betray him with such wickedness; it is a sin against God." She flounces away, but does not stop asking me to lie with her day after day.

Finally, one morning when none of the other men are in the house, she grasps me by my shirt and asks me again to lie with her. I flee, but she keeps my shirt clutched in her hand and shouts for help, telling the household "He tried to rape me!" When Potiphar comes in she tells him the same story and he throws me into his prison.

Even down in the dungeon I am fortunate, and feel God's presence with me. The keeper of the prison takes a liking to me, and puts me in charge of caring for all the other prisoners. I get to know two of them, a butcher and a baker who have somehow offended the Pharaoh.

One morning I notice that both men look troubled and ask, "Is something the matter?" It seems that they both have had disturbing dreams and don't know how to explain them. I say, "Interpreting dreams belongs to the Lord, but I will try to help you."

The butler tells me "I dreamed of a vine with three branches, with grapes on each one. I pressed them into Pharaoh's cup and placed it in his hand. What can this mean?"

"Listen," I said "The three branches stand for three days. In three days, the Pharaoh will restore you to your position and you will give him his cup again. But don't forget me when you go back to court. Please ask Pharaoh to get me out of this dungeon."

The baker likes what I told the butler and asks eagerly, "Will you explain my dream too? I dreamed that I was carrying three baskets of bread for Pharaoh on my head, but the birds were eating out of the uppermost basket."

I answer, "Again, the three baskets stand for days. I'm sorry to tell you this, but your dream means that in three days Pharaoh will lift up your head and hang you on a tree where the birds will eat your flesh. "

"O no," he cries, hanging his head in despair.

Three days later it is Pharaoh's birthday. He calls the butler and baker to him and the jailer tells me that the Pharaoh has restored the butler and hung the baker. But the butler must have forgotten to mention me, because I am still languishing in jail. Has God forgotten me too?

Two long years go by. Then early one morning the jail keeper comes into my cell. "Joseph, Pharaoh wants to see you. Right away." Then he brings me water and a fresh robe and helps me shave and clean up my appearance. "Maybe this is the day you've been waiting for."

I have never seen Pharaoh before. The Egyptians think of him as a god and I have to say he looks impressive wearing his tall golden crown and jeweled chains. Attendants fan him gently with palm leaves to cool him and keep away the flies. I bow deeply, and start to prostrate myself before him, but he stands and raises me to my feet.

"Joseph, my butler tells me that you can interpret dreams. I have had a strange dream that no one understands and I want you to explain it to me."

"It is not in me, sire. God will give you an answer."

"Very well. Now listen. I dreamed that I saw seven fat and sleek cows come out of the river Nile and start grazing. Then seven thin and gaunt ones followed and ate up the fat ones, but stayed as thin as ever. Then I saw a stalk of corn. It bore seven ears, full and good, and seven more that were withered and blighted. The withered ones swallowed the good ones. My magicians have no idea what all this means. Can you tell me?"

I pause to think a moment before I speak and then say. "Pharaoh's dream is one. It reveals what God is going to do. The fat cows and good ears stand for seven good years of plenty in the land of Egypt. The thin cows and withered ears mean seven years of famine, which will consume the land. Now, let Pharaoh choose a wise man to take charge of the food supply. Let him plan and store food during the good years to feed the people during the famine to follow."

Slowly, Pharaoh nods his head in agreement and asks his advisors, "Can we find such a man, in whom is the spirit of God?" Then he turns toward me. "No one is wiser than you. since you have told me all this. I shall set you over the whole land of Egypt. You will be second only to me in power and authority.

I stand there, stunned, as Pharaoh takes off his signet ring and puts it on my finger. Then his servants dress me in fine linen garments and hang a golden chain around my neck. Pharaoh makes me ride in his second chariot and gives me Asenath, daughter of a priest, as my wife. From that day on, I travel all over Egypt and see to the storage of food for the coming famine.

The seven good years pass, and the famine begins. We have stored great amounts of food, and when our people grow hungry Pharaoh sends them to me. I open the storehouses and distribute food carefully so it will last for the seven lean years.

Apparently Egypt is the only land prepared for famine, and before long, people from all over the earth start coming to us for food. One day I see some familiar faces in the crowd standing before me. Ten of my brothers, all but my younger brother Benjamin, have come down from Canaan to buy grain. I know who they are, but they don't recognize me in my Egyptian clothing.

I glare down at them from my raised chair as I consider what to do. Looking into my heart, I am surprised not to feel any desire for revenge. Over the years, my anger has melted away. On the other hand, I do wonder if they feel any sorrow for what they did to me. Have they grown and changed? I need to test them.

When I speak, I treat them like strangers, saying roughly, "Why should I sell you grain? You are probably spies."

"No, no," they cry, "We are from Canaan—ten brothers of twelve. One is dead, and the youngest is at home with our father. We just want to buy grain."

"Bring the youngest to me," I order. "Then I will believe you."

"That is the one thing we cannot do. He is the treasure of our father's heart since our brother Joseph died. He will never let him go."

Swallowing to cover the quiver in my voice I say, "Very well. You can spend three days in prison, and then we'll see what you say." When the three days have passed, I send for my brothers. "Let one of you remain while the rest go back with grain and get your brother. If you do this you will live."

They agree, and all but Simeon start home with their sacks of grain. I can imagine them begging my father, trying to get him to release Benjamin. It may be impossible, but we have reports of the famine growing worse and worse, and that may convince him. What good will it do to keep Benjamin at home only to have him to starve to death?

Finally one morning I see my brothers returning and Benjamin is with them. Praise God! I call my servants to prepare a feast and say that I will eat with them at noon. We gather, and I drink in the presence of Benjamin, the only other son of my mother, Rachel. I give him the best food and largest portions.

When it is time for them to leave, I tell my steward to put my silver cup in Benjamin's sack of grain. Then, after an hour or so, I send him after them. "Why did you steal my master's cup? You all must come back with me." It isn't long before they are standing before me again, protesting their innocence, denying knowledge of the cup.

"Very well then, all of you must empty your sacks so we can see." They untie their sacks, and immediately the shining silver cup falls out of Benjamin's sack.

"But I didn't take it," he cries.

"You, and you alone will stay and be my slave," I say.

Benjamin starts weeping, but Judah pleads, "My Lord, take me. My father cannot stand the loss of this favorite son. It almost killed him when Joseph disappeared, and this would be the final blow. He will die. Let me be your slave in his place."

My brothers have indeed changed. I can no longer control myself, and tears fill my eyes. "Let everyone leave the room except for the Canaanites."

The room empties and I call my brothers to gather around me. I weep aloud, in great gasping sobs. When I am able to speak again I tell them, "I am Joseph, your brother, whom you sold into slavery here in Egypt." I can see my ten brothers go pale, their faces aghast. "Now do not be angry with yourselves, for God sent me before you to preserve life. You did not send me here, God did, and has made me a ruler over Egypt. Go and tell my father, and bring him and all his household here to be with me."

Then I fall weeping on Benjamin's neck and he weeps too. I embrace all my brothers and we weep and talk together.

Pharaoh is glad for me and gives my brothers supplies for the journey. Soon our family is together again. Coming to Egypt gives my father a new lease on life and we embrace with the joy that comes only after deep sorrow and loss.

Our family settles in the land of Goshen, and lives peacefully together, but when my father dies my brothers are afraid again. They wonder if I will take revenge on them after all these years. I call them together and reassure them, "Fear not, for am I in the place of God? You meant evil against me, but God meant it for good, that many people should be kept alive."

And so my friends, when you think of my story with all its anger and evil and pain, remember the providence of God—how God was working behind the scenes all the time, bringing life and goodness out of hatred and evil. And when you remember, I pray you will dare to believe that God can bring good out of evil now, for you and for others, here in your town, your country, and even throughout the world.

5

FIVE WOMEN FOIL PHARAOH

(Based on Exodus 1-2:10)

Moses was such a handsome baby, with his thick dark hair and deep brown eyes, so full of life and sparkle. He would lie happily in his basket, studying his fingers and waving his pudgy little arms in the air. He was the apple of my mother's eye, and as his big sister Miriam, I helped her take care of him. Even father and our brother Aaron took time to play with him when they came in from their work. Moses lay at the center of our family and drew us together.

I still remember the shock and horror we felt on the day we heard about the Pharaoh's plan to get rid of us Jews. We were living in Egypt, descendants of Joseph and his family. Joseph had been honored as the last Pharaoh's right hand man. He devised a plan to deal with world wide famine, and later invited his whole family to come down to live in Egypt.

Everything was fine until the old Pharaoh died, but when the new one came to power, he didn't remember Joseph and was afraid of us. True, our numbers had grown, but I don't know why he felt threatened. We weren't planning a coup or anything. Finally he said to himself, "I can kill two birds with one stone. If I force the Hebrews to work on my building projects, I can get my pyramids finished and let the hard life kill off a bunch of them." So he enslaved our men and set them to work. But his plan backfired—our people were strong, and the more we were oppressed, the more we multiplied.

So Pharaoh moved to plan B, what you might call his "final solution." He ordered the Hebrew midwives to kill all the male babies as they were being born, but the Pharaoh didn't count on the courage of those women, Shiphrah and Puah. They feared God more than Pharaoh any day and dared to let the male babies live. Of course Pharaoh was furious, and demanded to know why the male babies weren't dying. Those two clever women bowed deeply before the ruler and said, "Oh great Pharaoh, we cannot obey you because the Hebrew women are so strong and vigorous that they deliver the babies before we even get to their birth stools. We can't do anything about it."

Pharaoh may have been skeptical, but he decided it was more efficient to issue a command to all his people. "You shall throw every boy born to the Hebrews into the Nile, but you shall let the girls live." Now our boys were in danger from all the Egyptians. Many babies died and our Jewish families lived in terror every day.

Miracles happened around Moses, and after he was safely born my mother managed to hide him at home. But it couldn't last. When he was three months old it was no longer possible. He was too busy and active to conceal any more.

Spies and Pharaoh's soldiers were everywhere, and we knew we had no time to waste. Frantic, my mother ordered, "Miriam, run to the river and get some papyrus, plenty for a basket, and some bitumen and pitch. Hurry!"

I gathered everything as quickly as possible and we got to work weaving a basket for Moses, sealing it tight with the bitumen and pitch so it would float. Then we lined the basket with blankets and laid our precious baby within it. We made our way down to the river Nile and hid the basket in the shallows, among the reeds where it couldn't be seen. Tears streamed down my mother's cheeks as she turned to go home. "Stay here, Miriam, and keep watch. I must go back in case the soldiers come."

Maybe my mother guessed something might happen, but I didn't know what I was watching for, except to keep Moses safe. Still, I obeyed gladly. I pushed through the tall prickly reeds and found a secluded place near the bank where I could keep my eyes focused on the place where we hid the basket. The sun filtering through the thick reeds warmed my face and I was beginning to feel a bit drowsy when I heard the sound of women talking and laughing. I peered out from my hiding place and saw Pharaoh's daughter, the princess of Egypt, surrounded by her ladies, approaching the bank of the river.

"Oh the waters will feel lovely on this hot day. I can't wait to bathe." The princess rushed ahead, removing her outer robes as she neared the river. She waded into the shallows of the Nile and then stopped suddenly.

"What is that over there in the reeds?" she asked her nearest attendant. "It looks like some sort of basket. Go and get it for me."

My heart seemed to stop. What would happen now? I froze and watched as the attendant waded deeper into the river and parted the reeds surrounding Moses. She reached in and drew out the basket.

I heard a tiny whimper, and the woman did too. "There's something in it, your highness. Something alive." Then she brought the basket through the water to the princess.

The princess leaned over and carefully removed the cover of the basket. "Oh," she cried, "it's a baby and he's crying! Poor little thing. He must be one of the Hebrew babies hidden here to escape my father's soldiers." All her women crowded around to look, but from my hiding place I could only see them and not the basket. Frustrating!

The princess gazed at Moses for a moment, and then she said, "I'm going to keep him and bring him up as my own son. I don't care what my father thinks." The women smiled as she picked Moses up and cuddled him in her arms. "I will call him Moses because I drew him out of the water."

Now was the time for me to act. Quickly, I made my way over to the princess and her women. They were all cooing and smiling at my little brother and he was beginning to smile back. I bowed to the princess and said, "Your highness, do you need a nurse for the baby?"

"Why I suppose I do. Do you know of someone?"

"Oh yes, I do. She's one of the Hebrew women. I'll go and get her right now."

I ran home as fast as I could, and found my mother. "Come quickly, Mother, the princess found Moses and she is going to keep him! She needs someone to nurse him."

My mother and I hurried back to the river and stopped before the princess. "Here is the woman I spoke of, your highness."

The princess smiled at my mother and said "Are you willing to take and nurse my little foundling? I will pay you generously."

My mother bowed deeply to the princess as she responded, "O yes your highness, I would be glad to take that responsibility." And so it was that my mother ended up being paid to care for her own dear child. And more, how little Moses, destined to become the nemesis of the Pharaoh, grew up right under his nose in the royal palace.

When Moses became a man, God called him to free our people. He reluctantly obeyed and went to face the Pharaoh. After a long struggle, the Pharaoh finally agreed to let us leave and Moses led our people out of slavery in Egypt. We were scarcely out of sight when the Pharaoh changed his mind and sent soldiers in chariots after us. How I rejoiced when we came to the Sea of Reeds and it parted to let us cross to safety, only to close again and drown the pursuing soldiers! Their chariots even got stuck in the muddy mire. I took a tambourine, and led the other women in dancing, singing a song of victory,

"Sing to the Lord for he has triumphed gloriously;
Horse and rider he has thrown into the sea." (Exodus 15:20-21)

We were on our way to the promised land!

* * * * *

Now let's leave Miriam, and think about this story. In her world, people thought of women as weak and of little account, but Moses lived and led the Hebrews to freedom because five women --four Hebrews who loved God and a baby, and a kind princess of Egypt—saved him. Five women foiled Pharaoh!

Full of drama and irony, no wonder this story is a favorite. Think about the difference that five women with no power except their initiative and courage made to the whole history of the Hebrews. In saving Moses, they saved the first great Hebrew leader and prophet, the liberator of his people.

Something deep inside us responds to the tale of an obscure slave child snatched from the jaws of death to serve God's plan. We admire the courage of the midwives standing up to the Pharaoh, the ingenuity and intelligence of the slave mother and daughter as they devise a plan to circumvent brute power. We wonder at the bearer of God's great purpose floating precariously on the Nile in a home-made basket sealed with a bit of pitch. We smile at the picture of the Egyptian princess offering Moses' mother wages to nurse her own child.

Perhaps most satisfying of all is seeing the child of promise delivered from Pharaoh's deadly hand by the gentle touch of his daughter. There is delicious irony in watching Pharaoh nurturing the life he most needed to destroy under his own roof. Moses is housed, fed, clothed, educated and protected in the palace, right under the nose of the ruler he will defy and defeat.

In the tale of Moses' rescue, we who are Christians hear echoes of another story we celebrate. A baby named Jesus is born in a rude manger, because there is no room for his family in the inn. Born a child and yet a king, he is immediately threatened with death by an evil ruler named Herod, and escapes just in time. Jesus and his parents travel away from the holy land, down to Egypt, in order to save him for his redemptive mission.

I think these stories appeal to us because so often life goes the other way. It's like a cartoon I enjoy: A humble little man is looking up at the heavens and saying, "Er, God, in case you haven't noticed, the meek are getting creamed down here."

According to Jesus, the meek will inherit the earth, but most of the time in our world they do get "creamed." This world crushes the innocent and tramples on the gentle. We want a reversal, please. Let's see the weak shame the strong for a change. That's what happens in Miriam's story. Five powerless women of intelligence, goodness and courage are the stars. Through their simple, unspectacular actions like protecting an infant, weaving and waterproofing a basket, coming to bathe in the river, answering a child's cry and finding a nurse, God's work was getting done. They rescue the liberator and position him to be trained for his mission.

This is no Cecil B. DeMille production or Stephen Spielberg spectacular. There are no special effects. It is simple and quiet, like snow falling on snow.

A story like this reminds us of our own power. Despite the enormity of the conflicts and struggles we face, the actions of ordinary people can make a difference now, just as they did for Moses. We are small, but we're big enough to make a difference if we will mobilize our courage and will. As British statesman, Edmund Burke said, "All it takes for evil to triumph is for good men (sic) to do nothing."

In closing, consider this story:

One morning at dawn a man went walking along the beach and noticed a woman ahead of him doing what looked like a graceful dance. As he grew nearer, he saw that she was bending down, picking up starfish that had washed up on the beach, and throwing them back into the water.

He asked the woman, "Why are you doing that?"

"Well, when the sun comes up high it gets so hot the starfish die."

"But what difference can you make?" he asked, "This beach is huge—there must be thousands of starfish."

"That's true," said the woman, as she bent over, picked up another starfish and threw it into the water, "but it makes a difference to that one." (story by Loren Eiseley)

I believe that God wants us to stop and bend over, picking up the starfish we see, doing whatever we can to help, wherever we can, instead of worrying about what we can't do, what we can't accomplish. We may not have to face a Pharaoh, but there is plenty of good work to do right where we are—service that takes the caring and courage of loving people.

The five women who foiled Pharaoh stand near the beginning of a long line of faithful people who lived courageously in faith and continued the story of God's salvation. May God keep us in hope and faith and courage as we make our journey.

6

THE RELUCTANT LIBERATOR

(Based on Exodus 2:11-4:17)

It feels so good to lie down in this cool grass and relax while the sheep are grazing. My father in law's flock and I have traveled a long way from our home in Midian--all the way beyond the wilderness to the mountain of God. The mountain is called Mt. Horeb, or sometimes, Mt. Sinai, because it lies at the apex of the Sinai Peninsula.

A soft breeze caresses my face and weary limbs as I let my mind wander back to the events that brought me to the land of Midian. I was escaping from Egypt after killing a guard who abused one of my Hebrew brothers. Even though I was brought up Egyptian, the adopted son of the Pharaoh's daughter, I knew that my real family, my people, were the Hebrews. The Pharaoh had enslaved them, and I couldn't stand the way he treated them. Then one fateful day I lost control when I saw a guard beating a Hebrew slave who wasn't working fast enough for his liking. He brought down the whip again and again on the poor man's back and I exploded. I rushed at the guard, hitting him with deadly force. I didn't mean to kill him, but when I saw he was dead, my heart filled with fear. I looked around and saw no one, so I hid the guard's body in the sand.

The next day, I saw two of the Hebrews arguing, and when I chided the one who was in the wrong, he said, "Are you going to kill me the way you killed that Egyptian?" Then I realized that people knew about what I had done. The Pharaoh's men would be after me, so I snatched some bread and water and left as quickly as possible. Even the princess could not save me from a charge of murder.

I traveled as fast and far as I could. When I came to Midian I sat down to rest by a well. After awhile, some young women came to draw water for their father's flock, but some rough shepherds came along and drove them away. Again, here were the strong abusing the weak. I rushed to the women's defense, and saw to it that their flock was watered and the shepherds left them alone. They thanked me, and taking their sheep, they turned and left for home. Before long, two of them came back to the well. They had told their father, Jethro, about the Egyptian who helped them—of course I was dressed in the Egyptian way—and he had invited me to come to break bread with them. I went back for a meal and ended up staying with the family for awhile, helping with the sheep. Before I knew it, Jethro offered me his daughter, Zipporah, as my wife. I agreed happily, so we settled down together and had a son we named Gershom.

Now my life is nothing like what I knew in Egypt, no pomp, no luxury, but a loving family and enough comfort for anyone. Every morning I rise from my bed, looking forward to a peaceful day caring for my father in law's sheep.

These reflections fill my mind and heart with gratitude as I sit up on the grass and look around to check on the sheep. They are all present and accounted for, but as I gaze at the scene, I am struck by a strange sight. A scraggly bush across from the place where I am sitting is glowing—no, more, it is actually on fire. As I watch, it begins to blaze. The flames burst out of it, reaching toward the sky, but the bush doesn't burn up. It isn't consumed in a normal way. How can this be? Leaping to my feet, I say to myself, "I must go and see why that bush isn't burning up."

Then I hear a voice calling, "Moses, Moses." It seems to be coming out of the bush.

In fear and trembling I answer, "Here I am,"

The voice orders, "Come no closer to the bush! Take off your shoes, for the place where you are standing is holy ground. I am the God of your fathers, the God of Abraham, the God of Isaac, and the God of Jacob."

I clamp my eyes shut and cover my face with my hands, for I am afraid to look at God. Everyone knows, that you cannot look at God and live.

Then God says, "I have seen the misery of my people in Egypt, and have heard their cry on account of their taskmasters. I know their suffering and have come to deliver them from the Egyptians, and to bring them out of that land, to a good and broad land, a land flowing with milk and honey. The cry of the Israelites has come to me and I have seen how the Egyptians oppress them. So come, Moses, I will send you to Pharaoh to bring my people out of Egypt."

What? I can't take in what God is saying to me, and protest. "But Lord, who am I that I should go to Pharaoh and bring the Israelites out of Egypt?"

"I will be with you," the Lord answers, and this shall be the sign that I have sent you: when you bring the people out of Egypt, you shall worship on this mountain."

"But, if I say to the Israelites that the God of their ancestors has sent me, what if they ask me your name"

I shrink back as God answers in a huge voice, "I AM WHO I AM! Say to the Israelites, I AM has sent me to you. Gather the elders of the people and tell them, The Lord, the God of your ancestors, the God of Abraham, Isaac and Jacob has sent me.' Tell them that I said,'I have heeded what has been done to you in Egypt, and I declare that I will bring you out of Egypt to a land flowing with milk and honey. They will listen to you, and go with you to the Pharaoh, the king of Egypt. Say to him,'The Lord, the God of the Hebrews, has met with us. Let us go three days journey into the wilderness that we may sacrifice to our God.' I know that the Pharaoh will not let you go unless he is compelled, so I will stretch out my hand and strike Egypt with all my wonders, and after that he will let you go."

My head is spinning. Visions of trying to convince skeptical Hebrews and standing before Pharaoh, the god-king, not to mention the thought of leaving my family and returning to a place where I am a fugitive wanted for murder, swirl through my imagination. How can I avoid letting any of this turn into reality? I rack my brain for a convincing excuse and cry, "What if they do not believe me or listen to me, but say, 'The Lord didn't appear to you.'"

I detect a note of impatience as God says, "What are you holding in your hand?" Glancing down, I see my shepherd's staff.

"It's just my staff."

"Throw it down," God commands.

I throw down my staff, and then draw back as it slithers away—a snake! But God says, "Grasp it by the tail." I seize the snake's tail, and lo and behold it turns back into my staff. "Do this," says God, " and they will believe I have appeared to you."

Then God goes on, "Put your hand inside your cloak and then draw it out." Now what? I do as God says and when I draw out my hand it is leprous, sickly white and scaly. Oh no! "Put it back in," says God. Quickly I do so, and when I pull it out it is healthy again. "If they don't believe you with the first sign, they may believe this one. If they still don't believe you, take some water from the Nile River and sprinkle it on the ground. It will turn into blood."

These magic tricks are certainly impressive, but I still don't think I am the one for this job. "O Lord, I have never been eloquent, but am slow of speech and tongue. Surely you want a good speaker for this great task."

The Lord's voice rose. "Who gives speech to human beings? Who makes them mute or deaf, seeing or blind? Is it not I, the Lord?

44

Now go, and I will be with your mouth and teach you what you are to speak."

"O my Lord, please send someone else."

Now God's voice is filled with anger, "What of your brother Aaron, the Levite? I know he is a fluent speaker. Even now he is coming to see you. Speak to him and put the words in his mouth. He will speak for you to the people. And take in your hand your staff, with which you shall perform the signs."

I am still trembling, but I know the conversation is over. God has had the last word. No matter what the danger, no matter what the cost, I am going back to Egypt.

* * * * *

Poor Moses. It's easy to sympathize with him. God is calling him to do a task that he believes is far beyond his powers. Not only does he lack trust in his abilities, but he is absolutely terrified. He will have to brave going back to Egypt, where he's a wanted man. Then he will have to stand before the Pharaoh, defying a ruler who is seen as god on earth. Moses will go, armed only with a simple shepherd's staff, and alone, except for his brother.

Though he doesn't feel it yet, we know that he is not really alone or unarmed—the presence, power and purpose of his God, are with him, guiding and upholding. We know that he will display amazing skill, creativity, patience and persistence as he forces Pharaoh to let his people go and then leads that recalcitrant bunch through the wilderness. We know that he will grow into a great liberator--the greatest leader and prophet the Hebrew people ever knew.

So we leave Moses for now, reluctant, yet poised to travel down to Egypt in response to a call he has heard and command he must obey. And now it's time to look at ourselves, traveling through these frightening early years of the 21st century. What is God's call for us?

The belief that God calls people to particular tasks and vocations is basic to both Judaism, and Christianity. From the hour that God called Abraham and Sarah to go out not knowing where they were to go, and to found a great nation, to the moment when Moses heard the summons to face Pharaoh in Egypt, to the day that the first disciples heard Jesus' call to "follow me" and St. Paul was struck down on the Damascus Road, countless people of faith have heard God's call—an inescapable call that must be heard and obeyed. They hear it still.

As Christians, we all are called to follow the will and way of our Savior, Jesus Christ. This is the vocation we share, whether our work is in the home or office, school or store, field or factory. God's call to us is rarely as dramatic as the one Moses heard, but like him, we are summoned to devote ourselves to God's purpose for our lives.

Living this way is not a chore. In fact it is the pathway to joy. Like investing ourselves in an activity we love, a good friendship or a loving marriage, the more we put into it the more we receive.

Still, a lot of us feel like Moses. We rebel. We prefer placing ourselves, our will, our goals and purposes at the center of our lives. After all, it's my life isn't it? Unless we think of life as God's generous gift, it's natural to think this way. Why should I squander my precious time, my hard-earned money, my life, on anything other than what I want? Why should I consider another agenda, much less the agenda of some mysterious God who makes arbitrary, unreasonable demands. Like Moses, we resist. Who are you, God, and what do I owe you? And more, what have you done for me lately? Just look at this messed up world of ours. Sometimes it's pretty hard to believe you're doing much of anything.

And like Moses, we have many excuses. How can we, unaccustomed as we are to public speaking, speak out for justice and mercy—and take on the Pharaohs of our day? You say you'll be with us, but where are the reinforcements—the chariots, troops, weapons. Send somebody else, anybody else, not me! What are you asking of me anyway? Are you saying you want me to risk—to risk my safety, my position, my comfort? To simplify, or sacrifice? To follow your call wherever it leads and do whatever it takes. You say you need me—with my particular gifts and talents and resources? That no one else wiil do?

The Chinese say that a journey of a thousand miles begins with a single step. Moses took that first step when he picked up his staff and set out for Egypt. We take it when we decide to respond to God's call in our lives and commit ourselves to partnership with God and each another in working toward a world of justice, compassion and peace

The call of God transformed Moses into a leader and liberator. He changed when he was faced with God's challenge. We, too, can be transformed by the renewal of our minds and become the people God calls us to be. We can live and love and serve the God of our life. May it be so.

7

MY HEART EXULTS IN THE LORD

(Based on I Samuel 1:1-2:10)

My heart exults in the Lord! My strength is exalted in my God!

If you had known me back in the old days, you would not have heard such words from my mouth. You would not have seen me as I am today, strong and filled with hope and joy. You would have known me as Hannah, the melancholy one; Hannah, the young wife of Elkanah the Ephriamite; Hannah, the barren one who could not bear.

It was so hard, so painful to be a barren wife. In our culture it is bad enough if a woman fails to bear sons, but to be totally barren is nothing less than a tragedy.

My family and I were so happy when the match was made with Elkanah. He came from a fine family, which pleased my parents, and he was a kind and gentle man, which pleased me. It was an arranged marriage, yes, but never just a marriage of expedience. We loved each other from the start, and felt blessed in our relationship.

But then the months and years went by with no babies... not even any pregnancies. It seemed that I just could not conceive. Everyone knows that children are a gift of God, and we wondered what we had done or failed to do to be denied children. My heart ached and Elkanah's did too, though he always tried to comfort me, saying, "Don't worry, God will bless us soon."

After several years had passed, Elkanah came to me, a sad expression on his face. He looked into my eyes as he took my hand and said, "Hannah, too many years have gone by without any children. It is my responsibility to take another wife who can give me children, but I promise that you will always be first in my heart."

My eyes welled with tears, and I stood silent for a long time. I knew that a good wife had to accept such a decision if she had her husband's welfare at heart—if she cared for the family's future. But how could I share him? How could I avoid hating the woman he would take to his bed? I felt as though the world were ending, my world.

Finally I said, "Yes. I know that it must be as you say." Then I hung my head and wept. Elkanah took me in his arms and kissed me more tenderly than ever before.

So it was that Peninah entered our home as my husband's second wife. It was a bitter time, and became even more bitter when the children started arriving, one after another. They were beautiful, healthy babies. I couldn't help loving them, but I was so envious!

In spite of all the children she gave him, Elkanah still loved me best, so Peninah grew jealous of me. He was true to his word and always treated me with special care. Peninah knew that she was only in our home to bear children and hated me more and more. She taunted me whenever Elkanah was not looking. "Why has God closed your womb? What secret sin have you committed? What's wrong with you, O barren one?"

I tried not to respond, to stay silent. What could I say? I had often wondered myself, "Why me? How have I offended God Am I being punished for some sin I don't know about?" Night after night I lay awake, brooding and praying, praying and brooding. I thought about the stories of Sarah and Rachel who bore sons late in life, but took no comfort in them. My faith and hope were sorely tested and I faltered more than once.

Now Elkanah was not only kind and loving. He was also a pious man, faithful in fulfilling his religious duties. Every year he made a pilgrimage to the shrine at Shiloh, where the ark of the covenant is kept. The ark contains the tablets of the law—the law which forms the basis of our people's life together. There Elkanah would worship and make sacrifices to Yahweh, our God. The whole family went along and made it a festive outing. It would have been festive, except for Peninah's constant picking at me.

One particular year, we left on our journey with a fine young animal to sacrifice. After the priests took portions of the meat for Yahweh and themselves, Elkanah gathered us all together to feast on the rest. He is so good and so generous—most men make the women and children wait until all they get are the leftovers—but Elkanah always includes us in the feast. The meat smelled marvelous! Elkanah gave each child a portion, and then handed me a double one of the very best pieces. This infuriated Peninah, and she started in on me again. Leaning over, she whispered, "O barren one...."

I just couldn't handle it. My appetite fled. I could not eat and my tears began to flow. Elkanah looked over and noticed my face. In concern, he asked, "Hannah, why aren't you eating? Why are you crying? Am I not more to you than ten sons?" Close as we were, why couldn't he understand? I jumped up and ran from all of them. Entering the quiet sanctuary, I threw myself down before the altar and began to pray. "O Lord of hosts, if only you will look on the misery of your servant and remember me. If only you would give your servant a son. I will give him to serve you all the days of his life."

Lying there, I prayed with all the faith and power I could muster. I didn't care if I was bargaining with God. I didn't care it my motive was selfish. I had to have a son and would do anything it took to get one. The meaning of my life depended upon it.

All of a sudden I felt a rough hand shaking my shoulder and heard an angry voice. "Woman, how long will you be drunken? Put away your wine." Puzzled I lifted my head and looked up at Eli, the old priest. Drunken? What did he mean? Then I realized that I must have been praying so intensely that my lips were moving. Eli thought it was drunken rambling, muttering to myself.

Scrambling to my feet, I explained," Please understand. I was praying—praying my heart out. I have been longing for a son for years and years but God has not opened my womb. Today I was promising to give my child to God if only I can conceive and bear a son."

As I spoke, Eli's expression softened. When I finished, he raised his hand in blessing. "Go in peace, and may the God of Israel grant your prayer."

When he spoke, I felt as though a great weight had been lifted from my heart. My despair dissolved and a sense of God's peace enveloped me. I thanked him, and went back to my family, calm enough to finish my meal.

When we arrived home from that pilgrimage, the sense of peace remained. I knew that there was hope, that God was with me. I would wait on God, trust God. Even Peninah's jibes didn't bother me.

Then came the joyous day when I discovered I was pregnant, and the even more joyous morning when our son was born—healthy and strong. We named him Samuel, which means "I have asked him of the Lord."

Elkanah and I felt much joy, yet it was tinged with sorrow. We knew that I must keep my promise and dedicate Samuel to the Lord. This meant that we would not raise him. We had to take him back to Shiloh to be raised as a priest. Legally, Elkanah could have cancelled my vow and kept our boy at home, but he respected the commitment I had made.

How I treasured the time I had with little Samuel. Most Israelite women nurse a child for two years, occasionally three. I told

Elkanah that I would wait to take Samuel back to Shiloh until he was three and fully weaned. Kind as always, Elkanah just said, "Do as you think best." Even so, the three years seemed to fly by. Before we knew it Samuel was weaned and I couldn't postpone taking him any longer.

I gathered all my strength and courage. I packed up Samuel's things and readied him for the journey. He was so very young! We set out with him, also taking sacrifices of flour, wine and a three year old bull.

As we traveled, I reflected on the magnificence of God's gift to us, this beautiful child—and I began to feel my sorrow turn to exaltation. It was so hard, and yet it seemed that the only way I could express the depth of my gratitude to Yahweh was by giving back our boy. Even if I had not made my vow, there was no other way. I felt so blessed—I wanted to give my dearest treasure, I was freed to give.

When we arrived at the shrine, we sought out Eli and I reminded him of our conversation so long ago. I presented Samuel to him, saying," Here is my boy. I have granted him to the Lord. As long as he lives, he is the Lord's."

It was done. The vow was complete, the decision, irrevocable.

How I had dreaded this moment! But Eli smiled and took Samuel's hand, receiving him gently. We said our farewells, turned, and left him there for the Lord. As we moved away, my baby reached out after us calling, "Mama." Eli calmed him and he did not cry. We knew that we would not see him for a year, but Samuel didn't understand that, or that he would not be living with us any more. We left quickly—I didn't want my baby to see my tears.

Before we started home, Elkanah and I went into the sanctuary to worship. When we knelt, I had expected to pray for strength, but instead I felt a sense of quiet joy. It was strange, but completing my commitment, sacrificing my beloved Samuel had left me feeling filled, not deprived. I burst into a psalm of praise. "My heart exults in the

Lord; my strength is exalted in my God. My mouth derides my enemies because I rejoice in my victory."

Something wonderful had happened inside me. It was as if all the terrible waiting to conceive, all the testing of my faith, the receiving of Samuel and giving him back—it was as if all these things had lifted me to a new level of faith and life. I returned home filled with joy.

After that, every year when we made our pilgrimage, I carried along a new little robe I had made for Samuel, having guessed at the measurements. How I rejoiced as he grew in stature and God's favor! Eli loved him and delighted in the way he learned so quickly and well. It made up for his disappointment in his own sons. They were supposed to be serving as priests too, but they were scoundrels, with no respect for God or their father. As Eli grew older, his eye-sight failed, and Samuel became his right hand man. He had all the makings of a fine and faithful priest. We were so proud.

The years went by and life was rich for us. You probably know that Samuel grew up to become a great prophet of Israel. And as for me, Yahweh opened my womb five more times and Elkanah and I rejoiced in three more sons and two fine daughters. No more tormenting from Pininah for me! We cherished all our children, but Samuel, that first great gift of God, was the one who taught me the depths of receiving and giving, of gratitude and sacrifice. Samuel always held a unique place in my heart. It was my experience with him that impels me to say, "My heart exults in the Lord."

Dear friends, it is my prayer that someday, maybe even today, you can say those words along with me, no matter what your situation in life.

I call you to dare to wait on the Lord, for our God is good and will act to save. I call you to trust fiercely, laying before God your heart's desire. I call you to wait on the Lord, and wait and wait, until at last you are lifted out of discouragement and despair into hope and expectation.

I call you to wait on the Lord, until you realize that all your blessings are gifts of God, and are freed to give back in gratitude and deep joy. Then your heart will know what it means to exult in the Lord.

8

CHOSEN AND CALLED

(Based on I Samuel 1, 3, 8, 9:27-10:1, 16:1-13)

I am Samuel, one of Israel's first prophets. Today, I want to tell you about two experiences that taught me how to listen and how to look.

Do you remember hearing the story of how I happened to grow up in the temple at Shiloh? Hannah, my mother, had waited for years to have a child. Her barrenness was a daily humiliation. Finally, in desperation, she promised God that if only she could bear a son, she would dedicate him to the Lord and have him brought up a priest.

Of course when I was little, I didn't understand all this, but when I turned three and we went to the temple, I certainly realized that my parents were leaving me behind. I will never forget entering the dim sanctuary and looking for Eli, the old priest. When we found him, my mother said, "My lord, do you remember me? I am the woman you saw praying for a child a few years ago--the woman who promised to give him to the Lord. The Lord granted my prayer, and now I have brought my son to serve God as long as he lives."

What was she saying? Did I have to stay here with this old man? "No!" I cried, throwing my arms around my mother's legs and hanging on for dear life.

Extricating me gently, she placed my hand in Eli's. I could see her eyes filling with tears as my father put his arm around her. His eyes were moist as well. Then they turned and walked away without another word. I started to cry, but Eli, the old priest, knelt down and held me, stroking my hair and murmuring soft words of comfort.

I didn't know what was going on, or why I was there, but Eli was kind, listening to my childish chatter and letting me stay near him as he cared for the temple and helped the people who came to sacrifice, worship and pray. I missed my parents keenly, but gradually my intense sorrow mellowed into a familiar but manageable ache. I knew my parents still thought about me and cared how I was doing. Every year, when they came to see me, my mother brought new clothing—always the right size--that she had made for me to wear.

The days, weeks and years passed quickly, filled with daily routines and tasks. In that temple I felt God's presence around me everywhere. And it was good that I was there to assist Eli, because his sons were no help. In fact they were scoundrels who had no respect for him, our priestly duties or even for God. On top of his evil sons, Eli had to worry about his eye-sight.

He could scarcely see, and counted on me to be his eyes. Before I knew it I was Eli's right hand man. Then one night a strange thing happened. Eli already had gone to bed in his room, and I was lying down in the temple, watching over the ark of the Lord, when I heard a voice calling to me. "Samuel, Samuel." Eli must need something, I thought, and ran into his room.

"Here I am, for you called me."

But he answered, "No, I didn't call, go lie down again."

I went back and made myself comfortable, but then I heard the voice again, saying "Samuel," so I hurried back to Eli's room.

"Here I am, for you called me."

"No, my son, I did not call you. Maybe you're dreaming. Go back and lie down." It was strange!

I lay down and it was only a moment before I heard the voice a third time. "Samuel, Samuel." Again I got up and went to Eli.

This time, he shook his head and looked at me thoughtfully. Then he said, "Go back and lie down. If you hear the voice calling again, say 'Speak, Lord, for your servant is listening.'" Did he think God was calling to me? I was just a boy.

I did as Eli said, and the Lord called to me as before. I answered, "Speak, Lord, for your servant is listening."

The Lord said, "I am about to do something in Israel that will make the ears of anyone who hears it tingle. I will punish the house of Eli because of his sons and their blaspheming."

I lay there trembling until morning. I was afraid. Even though I knew the Eli's sons were evil I did not want to say something that would hurt or anger him. But then Eli called to me and asked, "What did the Lord tell you? Do not hide it from me." So I told him everything, and he just said, "It is the Lord. Let the Lord do what seems good."

That night I learned to listen for the voice of God, and it was the beginning of a new life for me. As I continued to grow, the Lord stayed with me and did not let any of my words fall to the ground, lifeless and dead. God kept on speaking to me at Shiloh, and I kept on listening. I had to if I was going to communicate God's word to Israel. It was a huge responsibility, but gradually the people came to know me as a trustworthy prophet.

My leadership load grew heavier later when I became one of the judges among the people as well as a prophet. When they demanded a king, I had grave doubts. After all, God had always been the only ruler we needed. But they insisted on a king, and God told me to grant their request. It fell to me to anoint Saul as their leader.

As I feared, King Saul's reign ended in disaster and the Lord rejected him. I couldn't help feeling sympathy for this talented man who had fallen so low. But one day God said to me, "Samuel, how long are you going to grieve for Saul. Fill your horn with oil and go to Bethlehem, for I have chosen a new king from among the sons of Jesse."

"If Saul finds out he will kill me," I answered.

"To avoid suspicion, take along a heifer. When you get to Bethlehem say you have come to sacrifice to the Lord. Then, invite Jesse and his sons to sacrifice with you. I will show you what to do, and you shall anoint the son I name."

Then came my second great lesson in leadership. My call had taught me to listen for God's voice. Now I was going to learn how to look and evaluate from God's point of view.

And so it was that one bright blue morning I set out to find and anoint God's chosen leader in Bethlehem. When I arrived at Jesse's home we all went to the sacrifice. First, Jesse's son, Eliab, came and stood before me—a fine looking lad—and I was sure that he must be God's chosen one. But I heard God's voice saying, "Samuel, do not look on his appearance or his stature because I have rejected him. The Lord does not see as you mortals see; you look on the outward appearance, but the Lord looks on the heart." I had never thought of that before.

Then Jesse told his second son, Abinadab, to pass before me. Immediately I knew he was not the one, and said "Neither has the Lord chosen this one."

Altogether, Jesse made seven of his sons come before me, but when they were finished I had to declare sadly, "The Lord has not chosen any of these." I was puzzled, because God had told me that the new king was one of Jesse's sons, so I asked, "Are all your sons here today?"

Then Jesse said, "Well, there is still David, my youngest son, but he is out in the fields keeping the sheep. "

"Send for him. We will not sit down until he comes."

So they sent for David, the youngest son. After awhile he came, ruddy and breathless from running, yet handsome and with beautiful eyes. He asked, "What is happening?"

Then Lord said to me, "This is the one. Rise and anoint him." So I took my horn of oil, went to David and anointed him in the presence of his family. The Lord came upon him mightily from that day forward and later he became Israel's greatest king.

These two experiences of being called and choosing gave me two great insights--insights that have remained with me always.

That night God called to me in the temple taught me to listen for the voice of God and perceive it. After that I paid attention every day, listening and thinking carefully about what I was meant to do as God's prophet.

When God sent me to Jesse's house in Bethlehem I learned how to look, and to see in a new way. I realized that God's choice is not necessarily the oldest, the greatest, or the best looking. It might be the youngest, the smallest, or the humblest who is chosen for leadership and glory. God does not care about outward appearances. God wants us to look inside and understand a person's character. It is the heart that matters.

* * * * *

Samuel's story lifts up two great insights that guided him all through his life as a great prophet of Israel, and they can guide us as well.

The first is learning how to listen—how open your ears and heart to hear God's call in your life. I believe that God loves you and wants to communicate with you, no matter who you are or what you do. And more, I believe that God has something special for each of you to do—right here, right now, whoever you are, wherever you are. Probably your call will not come in the form of voice. More likely you will be attracted to doing something and then realize "Hey, this is for me. This is what I need to be doing." It can be anything from volunteering at the hospital or library or church, to playing the piano, gardening or fixing things or leading a group. Then, as you invest yourself in it, your interest and skill increase.

I believe the test of a true call is caring more and more about something you do. In my own life I felt called to ministry years ago, but was uncertain about whether it was really what God wanted me to do. I'd never even known a female pastor and wondered if I should stick to doing Christian education. But I have grown into the call and now I know that pastoral ministry was, and is, the right thing for me. I never dreamed I would still be preaching at the age of 80 but I love it more than ever.

Like Samuel, the first disciples and other biblical people, you can be called to some large task, some sort of creative work or leadership in the church or community. But a call can be something simple and quiet, like devoted praying for people you know, for the community and the world. The wonderful thing about being called to prayer ministry is that you can continue it even if you're confined or ill. Prayer was my husband Walter's ministry long after he stopped being active in other ways. He prayed earnestly for others until the day he died.

Following your call will enrich your life. All you have to do is open yourself, listen and follow.

Samuel's second insight has to do with evaluating ourselves and other people. God calls us to stop judging by appearances and to look deep into our hearts and those of others before drawing any conclusions. Good looks, well pressed clothing and perfect grooming don't matter much if our hearts are closed or mean or filled with hate. It is not right to take one look at people and dismiss them as undesirable because of an earring or tattoo, messy clothes, their color, nationality or religious affiliation. God looks past such things, searching for open and understanding hearts, filled with faith and hope, ready to accept, appreciate and love.

Today I pray that, like Samuel, you will learn to listen for God's call in your life, and to look at yourself and others God's way—past appearances straight into the heart.

9

YOU ARE THE MAN!

(Based on II Samuel 11 and 12)

INTRODUCTION

David was the most respected and glorified King of Israel. Conqueror of Philistines, unifier of the nation, psalmist, and forerunner of Jesus, he was the Jews' beloved and idealized king. Yet in today's story, we remember that like all of us, he was not perfect. The tale has enough sex, manipulation and violence to rival any 21st century drama or novel. Now hear this story of evil doing, judgment and repentance in the voice of David himself.

YOU ARE THE MAN!

I am David, King of Israel. You could say that I am <u>the</u> king. No other ruler is as revered and glorified as I.

Before I went to court I loved tending my sheep, singing psalms and playing the harp. Later, the sound of my harp soothed King Saul's jangled nerves. While I was only a boy I gained great acclaim for slaying the Philistine giant, Goliath, with my sling shot. When I came to the throne, my armies subdued the Philistines and recovered the Ark of the Covenant which they had stolen.

What a day it was when we brought the Ark back to Jerusalem! There is no more sacred object for us. The Ark houses the tablets of the law Moses received from our God, Yahweh, on Mount Sinai. Those holy tablets spell out our covenant with God and one another, and define our commitments and responsibilities. I remember dancing before the Ark, celebrating as both the political and religious leader of my people. Then God made a covenant with me, establishing the Davidic line forever.

I wish that I could say that those glorious days are all that I remember, but today I want to tell you about another time, a time which taught me that I am not the man I thought I was and want to be.

The story starts late one pleasant spring afternoon when I stroll out on the palace roof. I am standing there, enjoying the warmth of the sun and gazing out at my beloved city, when I look down at a nearby roof top and see a woman sunbathing. She is lovely, reclining there, her eyes shut, basking in the sunlight. Her gleaming dark hair falls loose around her shoulders, and I can't tear my eyes away. Immediately, I know I must have her as my own.

I call my servant and ask him to find out who she is. It seems that her name is Bathsheba and she is the wife of Uriah the Hittite, one of my soldiers away on the battlefield. "Oh well," I think, "it can't be helped," and send word for her to come to me.

My servant leads Bathsheba to my private quarters, and I take her in my arms.

You may ask, "How does Bathsheba feel about all this?" I have no idea how this beautiful woman feels, nor does it occur to me to ask. All I know is that I want her. She should be honored that the king desires her, and anyway, who is she to challenge the king's authority? After we have sex, she goes back to Uriah's home, and I think my pleasurable afternoon is the end of it.

But no. A few weeks later my servant brings me a message from Bathsheba. "Sire, I am with child."

What can I do? In our Jewish faith even the King is not above God's law. Right on our revered tablets of the law it decrees that a man must not covet his neighbor's wife.

My problem is that Uriah has been away for a long time. So I decide to have him brought home from battle on some pretext, so that he can sleep with Bathsheba. That way, no one will know that the baby is not his.

Uriah reports in and I encourage him to go down to his house, to his wife. But no, says Uriah, "How can I take comfort while my men are camping in the open field. Besides, O King, you know that sex is taboo while I am consecrated for battle."

The bottom line is that Uriah is too honorable to go to Bathsheba. Maybe if I get him drunk he'll change his mind, so I invite him to drink with me. But he still does not go down to his house, and sleeps alone.

It's too bad, but there's nothing for it but to get rid of Uriah, permanently. So I write my captain, Joab. "When you go back to the battle, place Uriah in the forefront of the fighting. Then draw back so he will be struck down and die."

Joab follows my orders, and before long he sends word that Uriah has been killed. I tell Joab, "Don't let this matter trouble you, Now one, now another, dies in battle. That's just the way it is." Encouraging him I add, "Press your attack and overthrow the city."

Bathsheba laments Uriah's death and I wait for the usual mourning period to pass. Then I take Bathsheba as my wife. Now I can claim the child she is carrying, even if it is born a bit early. It looks as though everything is going to be all right for me after all, and I breathe a sigh of relief. But I hadn't bargained for Nathan, the prophet of the Lord.

Nathan is the court prophet and has access to me whenever he has a message from our God. One morning, he comes and stands sternly before me. He bows low and says, "Listen, my king, I am going to tell you a story:

> "In a certain city there were two men, one was very rich and the other, poor. The rich man had many flocks, but the poor one had only one little ewe lamb. It grew up with the man and his children, eating their meager fare, drinking from his cup and lying in his bosom. It was like a daughter to him. A traveler came to the rich man's house, but the rich man didn't want to use one of his own lambs to feed the wayfarer, and took the poor man's lamb and prepared it."

I spring to my feet, exclaiming. "As the Lord lives, that rich man deserves to die; he shall restore the lamb fourfold because he did this and has no pity."

Nathan stands quietly for a moment, looking steadily into my eyes. Then he fixes me with his gaze and says: "You are the man."

I collapse onto my throne, slumping over as Nathan continues. "Thus says the Lord God of Israel, 'I anointed you king, I rescued you from Saul, I gave you your master's house and wives, and gave you the house of Israel and Judah, and if that had been too little, I would have given you more. Why have you done what is evil in my sight? You have killed Uriah with the sword and now the sword will never depart from your house. You have despised me and taken Uriah's wife to be your wife. I will raise up trouble for you from within your own house.'"

These true words pierce me like the sharpest knife, penetrating to everything I believe about being a servant of God, a good and just king, a good and just man. They function like a mirror, making me look at myself in a new and painful way. "I have sinned against the Lord," I moan.

Nathan answers, "Now the Lord has put away your sin and you shall not die. Nevertheless, by this deed you have scorned the Lord, and the child to be born to you shall die."

Without another word Nathan turns and strides out of the room, leaving me to cope with the evil of my actions, the death of my innocent child and Bathsheba's pain. I hang my head as the tears begin to flow.

* * * * *

In this great story of sin and repentance, David experiences the shock of recognition. He sees the inescapable image of himself at his worst—a rapist, adulterer, manipulator and murderer. There are no kind words for what he did, and he is condemned out of his own mouth.

We have to admire Nathan's courage in confronting this popular king. It's true that Israel's kings were not above the law like many eastern despots. David did not dare to kill Uriah openly and seize Bathsheba. But at the same time, the king wielded great power and it could be dangerous to accuse him. Nathan counted on the character of the David that he had always known and served.

We need to give David credit too. No Teflon for him. No trying to slide out of the problem. No squirming away from the relentless beam of prophetic light exposing his crimes. No passive acknowledgement, "mistakes were made." David owns his sin, and as a true king of Israel, he knows that his sin is not only against Uriah and Bathsheba and the moral being of his people. His sin is against God and God's holy law.

None of us likes to be called to account the way David was, whether our sins and shortcomings are large or small. None of us wants to be confronted with the worst about ourselves and our lives.

Consider the Peanuts gang. Lucy asks, "Do you think I'm a crabby person?"

Charlie Brown stops and thinks carefully. "Yes, I think you're a very crabby person."

What is Lucy's response? "Who cares what you think?"

Or, again, Lucy asks, "Do you know what the whole trouble with you is, Charlie Brown?"

For once, Charlie asserts himself and says firmly, "No, and I don't want to know. Just leave me alone!" He walks away, but Lucy yells after him.

"The whole trouble with you is that you won't listen to what the whole trouble with you is!"

It's true. We'd rather turn our backs and plug our ears than to hear "the whole trouble" with us. We have enough problems. Why should we listen to someone dissect us bit by bit? Whether we're kings or queens or pastors or presidents or just plain old people, we don't like facing the worst about ourselves. Even if the criticism is meant to be constructive, it's easy to respond with defensiveness or hostility. Anything to avoid that shock of recognition. Being able to listen and benefit from honest criticism is a gift, and it requires a large heart and soul like David's.

The minds God gives us are amazing. They can turn reality to our advantage—deflecting criticism, avoiding blame, protecting our view of ourselves. They are very creative in thinking of ways to avoid accepting the onerous responsibility for something we've done wrong. But the longer we hold responsibility at arms length, the longer we refuse to look at the truth about ourselves, the longer we stand under God's judgment, the farther we are from grace.

It is not easy to look at ourselves honestly when we're in the wrong. As one contemporary wag puts it, "The truth will make you free, but first it will make you miserable!" Yes, but facing the truth is the beginning of the journey toward freedom, forgiveness and renewal.

God's promise is that those who confess their faults will be forgiven. In order to change for the better, we need to see and deal with the worst about ourselves. Then we can pray for healing and the power to grow in grace Like King David before us, it is when we absorb the shock of recognition and confess our culpability that we receive forgiveness, turn around and move in a new and healthy direction.

10

OUT OF THE CAVE

(Based on I Kings 17:1-7, 18, 19:1-18)

I never asked to be a prophet, and believe me, it's no fun. I'm called Elijah the Tishbite, because I'm from Tishbe down in Gilead, but I don't feel that I have a home anymore. Prophets are supposed to speak truth to power, so I just go where our God, Yahweh, tells me to go and say what I'm supposed to say. That means I'm rarely welcome anywhere and always getting into trouble.

Take the first big job God gives me. I am supposed to go to the king of Israel—the king, mind you, not just some minor official.

Now you need to know that for a long time God has been getting angrier and angrier at King Ahab. His first mistake is not marrying a good Jewish woman. Instead, thinking it's good for international relations, he marries Jezebel, a powerful pagan princess of Sidon, who worships their god, Baal. That's bad enough, but soon Jezebel has Ahab worshipping Baal too, and that's a no-no for the King of Israel. Our God, Yahweh, is one, the only one, and doesn't take kindly to anyone who worships another god. Ahab does more to anger our God than all the kings of Israel who came before him.

God wants to lay down the law to this wayward monarch. So I speak the will of the Lord to him clearly. Word for word, this is how it goes: "As the Lord the God of Israel lives, there shall be neither dew nor rain these years, except by my word." Then I go off and hide to avoid the royal wrath.

After three years of drought and famine God calls to me again. "Go to Ahab, and tell him that I intend to send rain."

I go, and when I stand before Ahab he snarls, "Is it you, you troubler of Israel?"

"I haven't troubled Israel a bit, O King, but you certainly have, forsaking Yahweh and following the Baals. Now, the Lord intends to send rain. Have all of Israel gather on Mount Carmel, along with all the prophets who eat at Jezebel's table."

So Ahab assembles Baal's prophets and the Israelites on the mountain and I say to the people. "How long will you go limping around with two different opinions? If the Lord is God, follow him, but if Baal, then follow him." But the people don't say a word. They don't understand that Yahweh is a jealous God, unwilling to share their allegiance. So I decide to show them, and say, "I, Elijah, only I, am left as prophet of Yahweh, but Baal's prophets number 450. Let us prepare two offerings and lay them on two fire altars without lighting them. Then let them call on the name of their god and I will call on the name of the Lord, and the one who answers with fire is the true God."

The people agree, and I tell the prophets of Baal to go first. They build an altar and start calling out to their God and limping around and around their altar. They rave on until midday passes, but there is no voice, no response, no fire.

Now it is my turn. I call the people to come closer and drench the offering with water to make it harder to light. Then I stand and raise my arms to the heavens. "Lord God, let it be known today that you are God in Israel. Answer me, that this people may know that you are God, and turn their hearts back to you."

At that very moment, fire swoops down on the altar and consumes the offering, the wood, and even licks up the water around it. The people fall down saying, "The Lord is indeed God!"

"Don't let those false prophets escape," I order and the people seize all 450 of them and take them down to the Wadi to be slain.

I turn calmly to Ahab and said, "Go. Eat and drink for I hear the sound of rushing rain." Ahab leaves, but I stay at the top of Mt. Carmel, bowed down in prayer. Then the rain starts falling.

I'll never forget my victorious feeling on Mt. Carmel, that moment when Yahweh sent the fire swooping down to devour the burnt offering. Baal's prophets were defeated and slain. Yahweh reigned as Lord of the land again and I was his prophet. I felt the touch of the healing rain and it seemed that life could not be better. But then I have to head down the mountain to Jezreel, down to earth, down to the ugly reality of Queen Jezebel—her cruel spirit and her power.

Ahab has already told her everything—how the prophets of Baal are not only beaten, but killed, and how Yahweh has won the day. She is livid with rage, and out for revenge. Screaming "Where is Elijah, that wicked prophet?" she orders a servant to take me a message.

When he arrives, he trembles as he recites Jezebel's words. "Tell Elijah, so may the gods do to you, and more, if I do not make your life like the life of one of my prophets by this time tomorrow." I am a wanted man!

I know Jezebel means what she says, and tremble myself as I hear those words. My bones turn to water and my blood runs cold. Never have I been so afraid. Quickly, I gather up basic provisions—a little bread and water—and call my servant We flee for our lives, out of Israel, beyond Jezebel's reach, down to Beersheba in Judah.

The next morning I leave my servant and walk into the wilderness alone. My bread and water are gone. After traveling as fast as I can all day, I am exhausted and sit down under a lonely broom tree. I've had enough and cry out to Yahweh, "O Lord, let me die. Please, take away my life for I no longer want to live" Then I lie down under the broom tree, and fall asleep.

Suddenly I wake up, conscious of a firm but gentle touch on my shoulder. I hear a voice. It is an angel saying, "Get up, Elijah. Get up and eat." I sit up and look around, and there on a flat stone near my head are a warm cake and a jar of fresh water. I eat and drink gratefully, and lie down again. But again the angel comes and says, "Get up and eat some more. Otherwise the journey will be too much for you."

All I want to do is stop struggling and rest, but now I'm supposed to go on a journey? I get up and do as the angel says, eating and drinking as much as I can. It is wonderful food and I can feel the energy flowing into my body. Believe it or not, that meal keeps me strong for forty days and nights, as I journey all the way to Horeb, the mountain of God. There I come to a cave and lie down to rest.

In the morning, I hear a voice calling, "Go out Elijah. Stand on the mountain, for the Lord is about to pass by."

Then a mighty wind starts blowing, strong enough to split mountains and break rocks into pieces. But the Lord is not in the wind. After the wind comes a powerful earthquake creaking and shaking, but the Lord is not in the earthquake. And after the earthquake, a blazing fire, but the Lord is not in the fire.

When nature's tumult finally ceases, I hear nothing, nothing but the sound of sheer silence. This is the moment of the Lord. I wrap my face in my mantle, and stand at the entrance to the cave. There I hear a still, small voice saying, "What are you doing here, Elijah?"

"I have been working for you, O Lord, for the Israelites are forsaking you, throwing down your altars, and killing your prophets. I, only I, am left, and now they are trying to kill me."

"Go, Elijah, return on your way to the wilderness of Damascus. You are to anoint two kings, and you shall also anoint Elisha as prophet in your place. And you need to know you are not alone. I will leave seven thousand faithful in Israel, whose knees have not bowed to Baal and whose mouths have not kissed his image."

I knew it! The Lord has a plan, for me and my people. I am still the prophet of the Lord.

My fears drain out of me and I feel my heart swelling with new courage. I leave the safety of the cave and go out on my new mission.

* * * * *

Most of us can relate to Elijah's feelings after the contest on Mt. Carmel. He comes down to earth with a crash when he gets Jezebel's message—"by tomorrow I will have your life." He experiences what sports announcers like to call the slide from the triumph of victory to the agony of defeat and flees, heading south, beyond the reach of Jezebel and her death threats.

You and I may never have had to run for our lives, but we can understand the state of Elijah's mind and heart. We know what it is to do our best work, only to have it come to nothing. We have felt the grip of fear around our hearts, draining us of confidence and hope.

All of a sudden you are fired or laid off. You are faced with no job, no livelihood, and everything you have, your home, your car, your plans—stands under threat. Or your husband discovers that his body is riddled with cancer and the prognosis is dim. Fear for him, your family and future, crowd out your ability to function, perhaps even your faith. Will fear immobilize you? Or will you be able to keep going, to endure?

When Elijah is called to meet God, at first he is too afraid to go out on the mountain. He huddles in his cave as the wind, earthquake and fire run their course. But no God. After all the excitement comes the famous "still, small voice"—literally, the sound of sheer silence. Only then does Elijah cover his face and venture outside. As he stands on the mountain God's question comes out of the silence. "What are you doing here, Elijah?"

Elijah expresses his feelings, his hard work for the Lord, the sense that he is left alone and in danger. Even after meeting God, he is trapped in fear. God has fed Elijah, met and spoken to him, but it takes one more step to free him from the paralysis of fear. Like us when we're troubled or afraid, he wants sympathy, encouragement, and comfort. He'd love to crawl under the covers curl up in fetal position, and feel nice and safe.

But what happens? Instead of telling Elijah to take a good rest, go on vacation or at least get a soothing massage, the Lord issues new orders, gives him a new assignment. It's time for the prophet to stop wallowing in self-pity and get going. Only in action will he be healed, freed from fear.

God sends Elijah back into battle, and this time the job is even harder. He must pull off a double coup and anoint two kings, as well as calling and commissioning his successor. These assignments force Elijah to move past his own problems and focus on a mission beyond himself.

Then the Lord adds one more crucial piece of information. "By the way, Elijah, you thought you were out there all alone, didn't you? Well, you are wrong, I'm leaving 7000 people in Israel who have never bowed down to Baal. You are not alone."

The Lord takes Elijah's life all right, but not in the way the prophet meant. or the way Jezebel wants to. God wants the prophet's life freed from fear, ready to live and use in doing a new mission.

God's recipe for healing Elijah's fear is not complicated. It involves six ingredients:

1. Faithfulness—keeping track of us personally

2. Concern for our physical needs—food and rest

3. Presence—being with us in the dark caves of life

4. Communication—speaking out of the silence, offering the word we need.

5. Challenge—giving us assignments, sending us into mission.

6. Community—people on our wave-length with whom we can work and journey.

Will this recipe work for us, in our very different world? The answer depends on what we believe about God. If we stand with the biblical prophets in trusting that God is alive and actively involved in this world, working on an agenda of justice and mercy, and calling us to work on it too, we'll be able to receive the insights of Elijah's story.

If instead, we think of God as a mere concept or some sort of abstract force, who doesn't get involved in daily life or politics or care how we treat each other, if we think God's job is to make us feel good and be on our side right or wrong, if we think God only loves and never judges or expects anything of us, we might as well dismiss this story with its angels, voices, special effects and other hard to swallow ingredients. We might as well ignore its consuming fear, awesome demands and its vision of renewed strength and courage.

We are free to dismiss the story and stay huddled in our various caves. Of course we'll have to rely on ourselves when we're alone and afraid, but at least we won't have to worry about pleasing God, or anyone else except number one. We certainly won't have to go on some dangerous mission we didn't choose.

Once, Winston Churchill stood up to address a graduating class. He said, "Never give up, never give up, never give up." Then he sat down. That was his entire message. Are we able to conquer our fears and refuse to give up? Can we endure? Whether or not we embrace the cost and joy of discipleship is up to us. The choice is ours.

11

AT ODDS WITH GOD

(based on the book of Jonah)

INTRODUCTION

A lot of people find it hard to take the book of Jonah seriously. They get hung up on its historicity—especially the part about Jonah being swallowed by a big fish. And unfortunately, sometimes this is the only part of the story they know. So they ask, "How can a big fish swallow a man? Could such a thing happen? Did it happen?" It's too bad when people react like this, because they miss the point of a scriptural gem. Jonah is an artistic masterpiece, written not to stretch the limits of our credulity to the breaking point, but to jolt the Israelites—and us—out of intolerance and narrow nationalism, into an awareness of the wideness of God's mercy.

The book of Jonah can be understood as a parable. The story is set in the time before the fall of Nineveh in 612 BC, but it was written sometime after the Jews returned from their exile in Babylon, between 400 and 200 BC. It emerges from the reforms of Ezra and Nehemiah, which were undertaken in an effort to protect and preserve the Jewish heritage for a people which had been scattered and traumatized. The reforms were intended to bring the people back together again, but they also resulted in making them grow narrow and ingrown, suspicious of anyone or anything non-Jewish or foreign. They turned in on themselves, forgetting their ancient call to reach out as God's people and be a light for all the nations.

It is Jonah's story itself that offers us a revelation about God and God's dealing with people. You may remember the whole story, but now I invite you to hear it from the prophet himself.

AT ODDS WITH GOD

My life began comfortably enough. My father, Ammitai, was a prophet. He told me that my name means, "dove," which is an image for Israel as the bearer of a saving message for the world. Early on, I knew I was called to be a prophet too.

After growing up in Gathepher, I became a court prophet in Galilee for Jereboam, King of Israel. (I Kings 14:25) This job means I am supposed to be committed to supporting his view of life and politics. I am expected to keep things peaceful, not make waves like some prophets. On every issue I am supposed to say God is on our side. Even when the king wants to expand Israel's borders by taking lands of other peoples, I am expected to support him by saying it is the Lord's will.

Then, one fine morning everything changes. I am sitting quietly, just wondering what I want to eat for lunch, when Yahweh, our God, calls to me. "Arise, Jonah, and go to Nineveh, that great city, and cry against it for their wickedness has come before me."

How can this be? Nineveh is not our ally. In fact it's an utterly unsavory city, a symbol of the worst kind of cruelty and oppression. It's part of Assyria, which is dangerous, the arch enemy of Israel. At one point it conquered our northern kingdom and ravaged the south. Why in the world is Yahweh asking me to venture into the lion's mouth? Why should I, one of the conquered, try to preach to the conquerors? I wouldn't dare go there, and anyway, what good can possibly come of it.?

Then a horrible thought occurs to me. Yahweh is known to be gracious and slow to anger. Can it be that God might spare Nineveh if the people repent? I can't stand the thought. How can God even consider forgiving those terrible Ninevites? I certainly don't want to be party to their welfare. They are evil and need to be punished severely, even completely destroyed.

What to do? How can I avoid God's call? I stand thinking for a bit, and then call to a servant to my room. When he enters, I say, "Tell the king that I have to go away on urgent business and will be back as soon as I can."

"Right away." he says and scurries off with my message.

Quickly, I gather a change of clothing and a few other things I'll need and hurry down to the dock. The only way to escape Yahweh is to head off in another direction from Nineveh. I board a ship heading for Tarshish—the opposite direction—and collapse onto a bench, breathing a sigh of relief.

The first day of the trip the sun shines and the water is gentle and calm. The next day I see clouds beginning to gather on the horizon and the sky starts growing dark. Pretty soon the wind begins to blow in sharp gusts. It grows stronger and stronger and before long every timber of our little ship seems to be shaking and the waves toss it about like a toy. In a panic, the sailors rush back and forth, trying to row, bailing, taking down sails. Afraid, I go below deck, hoping to be safer there. Somehow I manage to fall asleep.

Then someone is shaking me. "Wake up, wake up." It is the captain "How can you sleep? Come, call upon your god, we've all been crying out to ours. Maybe your god can save us."

I get up and struggle my way onto to the shaking deck. It feels as if the ship is being torn apart.

"Someone's god is doing this," a sailors cries. "Who is the offender? What has he done?"

"Let's cast lots," another says, and we all gather around.

They cast lots, and horrified, I see that the lot has fallen on me. Everyone starts asking me questions. "Who are you" Where are you from? What is your occupation?"

So I tell them the truth. "I am a Hebrew. I am a prophet, and my God is the One who made heaven and earth."

Now they are terribly afraid. When I boarded I told them that I was fleeing the presence of the Lord, and now they ask "What is it that you have done?" We all know that this tempest is upon us because of me.

The wind is whipping violently as the storm grows worse. "What shall we do to you so the sea will grow quiet again?"

"Take me," I say, "and throw me overboard. Then the sea will be quiet for you. I know the storm has come because of me."

The seamen are not cruel and do not want to kill me. They row even more furiously, trying to reach shore. Their effort is in vain, and finally they raise their eyes to heaven. "Lord, we pray you do not charge us with innocent blood." Then they pick me up and toss me into the sea, and immediately the storm stops raging and the waves smooth out again.

I never learned to swim and am floundering in the waters, when all of a sudden I see the dark shape of a gigantic fish swimming toward me. What in the world? Then I see the great fish's mouth opening, opening, until it lurches forward and swallows me whole!

Darkness, deep darkness, but at least I am not dead. I lie back exhausted and shut my eyes. With no change in the light I cannot tell the time, but I when I waken I realize I've been sleeping a very long time. I sit up and pray to Yahweh, my God.

"When my soul fainted within me, I remembered the Lord; and my prayer came to thee, into thy holy temple....I with the voice of thanksgiving will sacrifice to thee;…Deliverance belongs to the Lord!" (2:7,9)

I feel the fish's muscles moving, like a great breath and an exhalation. Then I am propelled through its body and out onto dry land. I'm saved! Glory be to God.

But where am I, I wonder. It doesn't look like home. Then I see a little boy walking along the beach and ask the name of this place. "Why we're just outside Nineveh," he says.

As I am inwardly groaning, I hear something. it's a voice, God's voice, calling to me again. "Arise, Jonah, go to Nineveh and proclaim the message I tell you."

Obviously I have to obey this time, so I stand up and start trudging toward Nineveh, that great city, three days journey across. When I have traveled for one day I stop and cry loudly to all the people, "Only 40 days and the Lord will overthrow Nineveh."

The people stop and listen, and much to my surprise they repent, every last one of them, from the greatest to the least. They proclaim a fast and put on sack cloth and sit down in ashes. Even the king takes off his royal robe and joins them, saying, "let no one, human or animal, eat or drink. Let them be covered with sackcloth and let them turn from evil and cry to the Lord. Who knows, maybe God will turn from fierce anger and we will not perish." The scene is truly unbelievable.

But it is even more unbelievable when I realize God is actually going to forgive them. What a wimp! How can God decide not to destroy Nineveh after all the evil its people have done?

Full of anger, I pray to the Lord, "Isn't this what I was afraid of when I was still in my own country? I fled to Tarshish because I know you are a merciful God, slow to anger, and abounding in love. So now take my life, I beg you, for it is better for me to die than to live."

God answers, "Is it right for you to be angry, Jonah?" Not much of a response.

Sulking, I go to the edge of the city and make a booth for myself. I sit under it and wait to see what happens to the city. After awhile, a fine leafy plant grows up over the booth, and gives me shade from the fiery sun. It is wonderful—and I'd never seen anything grow so fast. But the very next day I see a worm attacking the plant, and before I can do anything it withers and dies. I feel very sad, it was a lovely plant and so useful for shade.

At dawn the next morning, a sultry east wind begins to blow, and without the plant the sun is beating down on my head until I feel faint. Again I pray to the Lord. "Oh Lord, let me die, it is better to die than to live."

God answers, saying, "Jonah, is it right for you to be angry about the plant dying?"

"It certainly is! I'm angry enough to die myself."

"Jonah, you pity the plant, for which you did not labor, nor did you make it grow, which came to being in a night and perished in a night."

Only then do I realize that God must have sent the plant.

The Lord continues, "If you pity the plant, should I not pity Nineveh, that great city, in which there are more than a hundred and twenty thousand persons who do not know their right hand from their left, and also much cattle?"

"Why shouldn't God take pity?" Stunned, I know I must think about that question, and never forget the kind of merciful God I serve.

* * * * *

We need to think about God's question too, "Why shouldn't I take pity?" It is the basic, searing question posed by the story, placed with artistic perfection at the very end, so it challenges not only Jonah and the intolerant Jews of the post-exilic period, but also you and me. God's question forces us to examine our hearts.

If God is universal, the Creator of all, and if God's purpose is to enter into a saving relationship with humanity, why is it so tempting to claim that God's love and care belong to us? Why do we tend to think of God's love as being especially for our kind, our faith, our nation? Why do we resist or resent the thought that God's love might extend to people we don't care for, who flout our standards or disagree with our ideas and values? Why does it seem important to set limits on God's love and salvation in keeping with our understanding of justice?

Why is it so easy to be what Harry Overstreet called the "gentle people of prejudice"—to hate *en masse* the way the Jews hated the Gentiles and vice versa—to quietly and courteously write off a whole class or group of fellow human beings? How can some of us be willing, even eager, to think of some other people as being damned?

I have heard some Christians say that it would be a violation for God to choose to save non-believers. After all, doesn't scripture insist that we must believe in the Lord Jesus Christ to be saved? We have believed, they say. We have behaved as we ought. How could God let us "good" people down and extend salvation beyond the boundaries of our understanding? Surely God won't break the divine rules and commands we have been taught.

Just as Jonah can rejoice in the impending destruction of Nineveh, there is something in many of us that lets us be glad when people we frown on "get theirs." It is more than booing the villain in a melodrama or taking delight in seeing justice done. It is an enjoyment in seeing the "bad guys" suffer. It is delighting in punishment without hoping for growth, change, rehabilitation or redemption.

As Christians, if or when we feel this ugly delight creeping into our minds and hearts, we are called to confess it. It is a sure sign that we have forgotten that we are all "bad guys" to one degree or another—mixtures of good and evil. It confronts us with the reality that we are all sinners. As St. Paul put it, "...there is no distinction, since all have sinned and fall short of the glory of God." (Romans 3:22b-23)

We are rather like the unforgiving servant in Jesus' parable—the one who is forgiven a huge debt only to turn around and refuse to forgive someone who owes him only a small amount. We fail to forgive as we have been forgiven. (Matthew 18:23-34)

Haven't you noticed how easy it is to be gentler with ourselves than others? It's not that hard to be understanding when you, or someone you love, does wrong. There are so many reasons and extenuating circumstances. Surely we deserve mercy. But when it comes to someone down the block, in the ghetto or even another neighborhood, anyone outside our circle of caring, we say, "Throw the book at them."

This is the spirit of Jonah—preferring punishment to salvation, moralizing to forgiving. It is the spirit we succumb to when we resent the possibility of God forgiving people we perceive as sinners or enemies. Our targets vary, but when we look honestly and deeply within ourselves I would wager that all of us have at least one person or group we'd just as soon see consigned to hell. We see them as wayward, sinful, destructive or just plain wrong. We draw lines between good and evil, us and them, and want to believe that God sees things the same way we do.

If we catch ourselves doing this, we need to face the fact that, like Jonah, we are standing against God's reconciling, redemptive purpose. Adamant and unforgiving, we are at odds with God. We are giving the wrong answer to God's question, "Why shouldn't I take pity?" Why shouldn't I forgive?

As Christians, we are challenged to ask <u>ourselves</u> God's question. Why shouldn't I take pity? Why shouldn't you? Why shouldn't we seek to enlarge our capacity for forgiveness and compassion instead of judging harshly and taking delight in punishment? Do we not follow a Lord who came to seek and save the lost? A Lord who delights more in one little lamb who is lost and found than in 99 who stay home? (Luke 15:1-7) Don't we follow a Lord who came to reveal God's compassion on all people?

The powerful message of Jonah calls us away from narrowness of heart and spirit into larger compassion and awareness of the mercy and generosity of God. It foreshadows the Gospel in picturing the God of the good news who asks not "why shouldn't I condemn?" but "why shouldn't I take pity?" Is this God of ours soft on sin? By no means. Our God is the God who hates sin, but loves sinners—you and me and the whole human family. Thanks be to God!

12

A NEW FAMILY

(Based on the book of Ruth)

Famine was ravaging Bethlehem when Naomi and Elimelech moved to our to our country of Moab. At first they kept to themselves, and I heard they didn't plan to stay any longer than necessary. But days turned into months, and months into years, and they settled down among us. As we came to know them and their sons better, it was interesting to notice their customs—more sophisticated than our country ways.

Then one day, tragedy struck the couple. Elimelech died suddenly in Naomi's arms. She was crushed, and leaned heavily on her two sons, Chilion and Mahlon. The young men were of an age to marry, and they began to visit my sister Orpah and me, Ruth. Before long our families got together to discuss betrothal, but I had the feeling that Naomi didn't think much of us. She probably wanted her boys to go back to Judah to find Jewish wives, but by then it was too late. My sister and I were betrothed to her sons, and ready to marry.

After the double marriage ceremony, Orpah and I moved into Naomi's home with our husbands. She was standoffish at first. I think she thought we didn't know how to do much of anything. Well, I guess we didn't, from her point of view, because we did things differently. We wanted Naomi to like us, and listened carefully when she told us how to make the dishes our husbands enjoyed eating. We tried to clean and dress the way she did too.

Soon, Naomi seemed to notice the effort we were making and warmed to us. In the evenings she invited us to sit and listen to her stories. She told us of her people, the Israelites, and the bitter suffering they experienced in Egypt. Then she went on to tell the wonderful story of how God led Moses and the people on the Exodus through sea and wilderness, all the way to the promised land. I began to think of the children of Israel as my own people.

Ten good years passed. Neither Orpah nor I had been blessed with children, but we were all living happily together. Then one horrible day, both of our husbands came down with a ravaging fever that took them in a matter of hours. Stunned, we three women stood paralyzed with grief. All the men in our lives were gone now. All gone. It was unbelievable.

When we began to be able to think again we sat down and talked about what to do. You may know that widows, and all women without men, have few choices in our world. Naomi said, "I have heard that God has been kind to my people in Judah. Food is no longer a problem. We could all go to Bethlehem and be with my kinsfolk there." Orpah and I agreed, and we began to prepare for the journey.

The day of departure dawned and we started out toward Judah. Before we had traveled far, Naomi stopped short and turned to us. "Ruth, Orpah, this is wrong. It is not right for me to take you away from your homeland. Go back to your families, my daughters. They will help you find security with new husbands." Then she put her arms around us tenderly and kissed us.

In silence, we stood embraced for a few moments. Then we both cried out "No. We will go with you to your people."

Naomi's eyes filled with tears as she smiled and said gently, "My dears, I have no more sons to give you and I am too old to have another husband. Even if I found a husband tonight and had more sons, would you wait for them to be grown? Go back, the Lord's hand has turned against me."

We all wept. Then Orpah kissed our mother in law, and turned to go back home, but I clung to Naomi. "Entreat me not to leave you or turn back from following you! Wherever you go, I will go; wherever you lodge, I will lodge. Your people shall be my people and your God, my God. Where you die, I will die—there will I be buried. May the Lord do thus and so to me, and more as well, if even death parts me from you."

Naomi gazed deeply into my eyes and I met her gaze steadily. She said no more, but clasped my hand. Together we turned and moved off toward her homeland.

We arrived in Bethlehem when the barley harvest was in full swing. People were amazed to see Naomi again. They welcomed us, but she was feeling very low, saying. "I went away full, but have come back empty."

Hoping it would lift her spirits, I asked if it would be all right for me to go and glean grain behind the reapers. That way we would have better food and I might find favor with someone who had property. She agreed and I made my way out to the fields and asked to glean.

Gleaning was hot, exhausting work, but after awhile my sack began to swell with what I had gathered. As the noonday sun blazed down on us, an imposing looking man strode into the field. It seemed that he had just returned from town. One of the other gleaners whispered to me, "It is Boaz, the owner of these fields.

Boaz moved slowly among the reapers, checking their work. He greeted them as he went from group to group, "Bless you, that's good work, God bless you."

The reapers responded in kind saying "Bless you, sir." They seemed both to like and respect him.

Then Boaz turned and noticed me. He asked the servant in charge of the reapers, "That young woman gleaning over there—whom does she belong to?"

I could hear the servant answer, "That is Ruth, the Moabite, who came back from Moab with your kinswoman, Naomi. She came here early this morning and asked if she could glean behind the reapers. We agreed and she has been here all day, on her feet without any rest at all."

Then Boaz walked over to me and said, "My daughter, stay here in this field, near the young women of my household. I have ordered the young men not to bother them, and if you get thirsty, drink from the water they have drawn."

I fell down before him and asked, "Why have I, a foreigner, gained favor in your sight?"

"I have been told of all you have done for your mother in law, Naomi, since the death of your husband—how you left your father and mother and native land for her sake and came to a people you did not know before. May the Lord reward you, the God of Israel, under whose wings you have come for refuge."

I could scarcely believe such kindness and answered "May I continue to find favor in your sight, my Lord, for you have comforted me and spoken kindly to your servant, though I am not your servant."

Later, at mealtime, Boaz invited me to sit beside him and the reapers. He handed me a fine piece of bread and said, "Here, take this bread, dip it in the wine and eat. Then he piled grain high on my plate. I took it and ate my fill, and there was some left over.

As I sat there eating, I heard Boaz saying to the men, "Let Ruth glean even among the standing sheaves, and pull out some handfuls from the bundles and leave them for her to glean. And do not reproach her." Amazing!

So it was that I gleaned in that field until evening, and went home carrying about an ephah of barley—that's a little over a bushel. Naomi was thrilled, and took out all the grain she wanted to eat. She hadn't had enough food in a long time.

When she was satisfied, Naomi asked me all about where I worked and the man who noticed me. I told her, "His name was Boaz."

Why Boaz is one of our nearest kinfolk." Naomi exclaimed. "Stay near his young women and you will be fine."

And so it was that I went out to the fields daily, staying close to the young women of Boaz' household and gleaning until the end of the barley and wheat harvests. In the evenings I went home to Naomi and we had enough to eat every day.

That would have been enough, for us who had been hungry for so long, but the Lord God of Israel blessed us even more. Boaz redeemed Elimelech's property from Naomi, and made me his wife. Together we had a son named Obed, who comforted Naomi in her old age, and became the father of Jesse, who became the father of David, the greatest king of Israel. What an honor to be part of that new family! Praise be to God!

* * * * *

When the Jewish people returned from exile, they grew rather ingrown and narrow. They kept to themselves and were suspicious and prejudiced against outsiders and foreigners. The story of Ruth was told to remind them that God was not their private property. Their God is the God of all nations and peoples, not just Israel. Moabites like Ruth, stand within the circle of God's care just as much as they do.

The story stretches the understanding of family too. In Ruth's time it was unheard of for a widowed woman from one land to stay with her foreign mother in law instead of returning to her blood relatives. Such a thing was shocking. Still, Ruth felt the sense of family even more strongly with Naomi, who was not of her blood but was of her heart.

Ruth's story foreshadows the teaching of the Jesus and New Testament. When Jesus asked, "Who is my family, my brother, sister, mother?" he redefined family by saying, "Those who hear God's will and do it."(Mark 3:31-35) The family Jesus created was built on faith and commitment, not blood.

The family of Christ, the family called church, grew and developed it became more and more inclusive, reaching out to affirm the teaching that God has made all nations of one blood.

Even though this radically inclusive vision of God's family has been with us for a long long time, sometimes we forget. Sometimes we want to huddle together with our own kind. Sometimes we want to ignore or exclude or even condemn those who are different. The story of Ruth is for us too—as a continuing reminder that God's love and care embraces everyone everywhere—no exceptions.

NEW TESTAMENT
VOICES

1

MARY'S SONG

(Based on Luke1 and Matthew 2:18-25)

That morning I was alone in the house. My father was working outside, and my mother had taken some food to a sick neighbor. My younger brothers and sisters were scattered about doing their chores. I was sitting in my room, mending a shirt and enjoying the bright sunlight pouring through my window and warming my skin. What a beautiful day!

I fell into a kind of reverie as I sat there sewing. As my fingers worked the needle in and out of the fabric, my mind traveled to thoughts of Joseph, my betrothed. A month ago, right after my thirteenth birthday, we had taken the traditional first step toward marriage in a formal ceremony. Right here in our house, we stood in front of our rabbi, family and friends and promised our lives to one another. From that moment on we were considered husband and wife even though I would live at home for another year. Our marriage would be complete the day Joseph took me to his home and we established our own household. How I dreamed of that day! But already I belonged, not to my father, but to Joseph. I felt so fortunate to be betrothed to a man like him, strong and gentle, kind and just. God truly had blessed me.

As these thoughts flooded my heart I felt the sunlight growing warmer and brighter around me. I looked up and saw a brilliant, blinding light, like none I'd ever seen before. Then I heard a voice saying, "Hail, O favored one, the Lord is with you."

I jumped, startled and afraid, but the voice went on, "Fear not, Mary, I am God's messenger, the angel Gabriel, and you have found favor with God. Behold, you will conceive in your womb and bear a son, and you will name him Jesus. The Lord God will give him the throne of David; and there will be no end to his kingdom."

I listened in wonder and confusion, and asked the angel, "But how can this be, when I have had no relations with a man?"

Gabriel answered, "The Holy Spirit will come upon you, and power from the Most High will overshadow you. Therefore the child will be called holy, Son of God. And now, your relative, Elizabeth, despite her age and barrenness, has also conceived a son, and is in her sixth month of pregnancy. For nothing will be impossible with God."

My heart filled with awe. How did I find favor with God? Of course every Hebrew woman hoped she might be the one to bear the Messiah we wait for, but why would God choose me to bear this child—just a young girl, a nobody? My family has no power or riches. In fact we are part of the people called *anawim*, poor ones who depend totally on God.

But how could I question God's messenger? If Gabriel said this was what God wanted of me I had to take it seriously. I closed my eyes and sat very still, thinking about God's call to me. I knew that God doesn't force people to obey and wanted me to choose. But what would it mean to say yes? It was hard to think of this call as a sign of favor. If this was favor what would God's disfavor be like? I knew that saying "yes" would be very difficult, and terribly dangerous.

Questions tumbled through my mind, one after the other. How could I tell my mother and father I was going to have a baby when I had not yet gone to Joseph's home and made love with him? And what would Joseph say? Would he think I had betrayed him with another man? Would he exercise his right as my betrothed and have me punished for adultery? The punishment was stoning, and they would stone me until I was dead. But no, I must not think of that. I dared not let fear capture me. I had to trust God's wisdom. If the God who has always blessed me wants me to do this, I must say "yes."

I lifted my face to the light and said to Gabriel, "Behold the servant of the Lord. Let it happen to me according to God's word."

The brilliant, blinding light faded, and left natural sunlight pouring through the window. My room looked the same, with the same worn furniture, the shirt I was mending still sitting on the table waiting for me to finish fixing it. Everything looked the same, yet my whole world, my whole life, was different, interrupted by the call of God.

At first I didn't know what to do next, but I knew I had to talk with someone, someone who would understand. But who? Then I thought of Elizabeth. The angel had said she, too, was anticipating an amazing birth. Surely she was the one.

I put away my mending and scribbled a brief word to my mother saying I was going up into the Judean hills to visit Aunt Elizabeth. Mother might wonder, even worry, but there was no help for it, I had to go.

My idea that Elizabeth was the one I needed to talk with was perfect. When I knocked, and she saw me standing at her door, immediately she knew something wonderful was happening to me. "Blessed are you among women, Mary, and blessed is the fruit of your womb. The moment I heard your greeting, the babe in my womb jumped for joy."

Then she sat me down and asked for the whole story. By the time I finished telling her about the angel's visit and the child I had agreed to bear, my heart was overflowing with gladness. It was as if I realized fully what God was doing, not only in me, but for our whole people. This child of mine would be the Messiah we've been waiting for. God's salvation was entering history with power the way it did long ago when we escaped from slavery in Egypt. God was making the impossible possible! A song of amazement and praise flowed from my lips:

> My soul magnifies the Lord, and my spirit rejoices in God my Savior, who has looked with favor on the lowliness of his servant. Surely, from now on all generations will call me blessed, for the Mighty One has done great things for me, and holy is God's name. (Luke 1:46-49)

I didn't go right home, but stayed with Elizabeth for three months. She wrote to my parents about my pregnancy, in the hope they would understand. They neither understood, nor believed my story, so it was painful when I arrived back home. My parents were deeply wounded, but they loved me, and vowed to do their best to protect me from harsh punishment.

I still had to face Joseph and went to see him right away. When I told him what had happened in my room that morning he seemed more sad than anything else. He spoke slowly and deliberately, without meeting my eyes, "This breaks my heart, Mary, I never dreamed you would betray me. Please don't make it worse by making up some wild story about angels and finding favor with God. At least do me the honor of telling the truth."

Finally he looked into my face, his eyes brimming with tears. "Go now, Mary, I have to be alone. I must think and decide what to do."

My cheeks were drenched with tears as I turned and ran from Joseph's house. I couldn't stand the hurt and pain exuding from his every pore. If only he believed me; trusted that I was telling him the truth. What would he decide to do? Would this man who loved me accuse me of adultery and have me stoned? I knew he had every right to do so.

Later that day Joseph came to the door and called me outside. "I just want you to know, Mary, I have made my decision. I can't bear to disgrace you publicly or to have you stoned. I've decided to divorce you quietly and go away. Perhaps someday I can put my life back together. I hope you will be able to as well. Goodbye, Mary."

I put up my hand tentatively, as if to touch his arm, but he brushed it aside, turned and strode away without another word. As I watched his figure receding down the road, I whispered, "Goodbye, Joseph, goodbye my love," Then I sank down to the ground and wept sobs of despair. I still believed I had done right to say "yes" to God, but the joy I had felt with Elizabeth dissolved in the sorrow of losing Joseph. What would I do now? What could I do? I went inside and told my parents about Joseph's decision. They were sad too, but relieved to know I was safe from stoning.

That night I went to my room, the same room once filled with God and light. I fell to my knees beside my bed and tried to pray. "O my God, if I have found favor with you, please help me now. Please guide me and show me the way." Then I lay down, shut my eyes and tried to sleep.

I must have dozed off because I awoke to loud knocking and my mother's voice calling. "Mary, Mary. Wake up."

I jumped up and opened the door. "What is it mother, is something wrong."

"I don't know, but this morning when I looked outside, there was Joseph, sitting under our olive tree. You said he had left for good, so I thought I should get you instead of inviting him in."

What could he be doing here? I threw on my clothes, smoothed my hair, flew to the front door and flung it open. The sun was high already, heating up the day. I looked out, and sure enough, there was Joseph, sitting in the shade of our old olive tree. For a moment I just stood there, wondering what to think, what to do. Was his presence good news,... or not?

Then Joseph saw me and got to his feet. He moved toward me with arms and hands extended and his mouth upturned in a smile.

Joyfully, I ran to meet him and he wrapped me in his arms. "Mary, Mary, I'm sorry, so sorry I did not trust you. Can you ever forgive me? Come, let me tell you what happened to me last night."

Keeping an arm tight around my shoulders, as if he were afraid to let me go, Joseph drew me over to the olive tree. We sat down side by side and he told me his story.

"Yesterday, after I said goodbye to you and went home, I was utterly exhausted. I lay down to rest and think about where and how I would make a new start. I must have fallen asleep, because I began to dream. I saw a blinding light, Mary, more brilliant than any I had ever seen.

"It was an angel! He said 'Do not be afraid to take Mary as your wife, Joseph. The child she is carrying is from the Holy Spirit. She will bear a son, and you are to name him Jesus, for he will save his people from their sins. This will fulfill Isaiah's prophecy: "Behold, a virgin shall conceive and bear a son, and they shall name him Emmanuel, God with us.' Then I awoke, and realized how terribly I had misjudged you. Please Mary, forgive me, and if you can forgive me, let me be your husband."

I should have known that the God who makes the impossible possible would make Joseph understand what had happened to me. I reached out, took his hand and held it up to my cheek, stroking its work-roughened skin.

"Of course I forgive you Joseph. I just praise God for showing you the truth and for giving you back to me."

We began to make plans. I would go to Joseph's home right away to stop any gossip and cruel talk. We would start building our life together and get ready for this wonderful baby who was coming to save us all.

You know the rest of the story.

*The long, uncomfortable trip to Bethlehem for the census, the birth in a cave behind the inn, the shepherds and animals and later, the wise-men.
*The journey to Egypt to escape Herod's murderous plans for Hebrew toddlers.
*The visit to the temple when Jesus was eight days old, when ancient Anna and Simeon warned us that our dear child would die, a sword piercing our hearts.
*Life in Nazareth, bringing up Jesus in Joseph's carpenter shop.
*Jesus' three year ministry of preaching, teaching and healing.
*His arrest and trial and death on a cross between two criminals.
*The glorious day of resurrection and the beginnings of the church.

I've spent many years pondering my story--the fears and challenges I've faced and embraced--the comfort and strength God has given me. I don't know what fears you are facing today, or what you are up against in your life, but I do know that you can trust God to guide you through and turn your weeping into laughter. You can dare to believe Gabriel's promise, "With God, all things are possible," Praise be to God!

2

ACCEPTANCE—A WORD FROM JOSEPH

(Matthew 1:18-25, Luke 2:1-5)

One of life's greatest challenges lies in accepting what comes to you. It is not easy. Sometimes reality, the way things are, seems so bad that it's utterly unacceptable. You're absolutely unwilling to live with it.

You feel angry and out of control.

Maybe something happens to your health, or the health of someone you love. Suddenly you're faced with an illness or disability you can do nothing about. Perhaps your grown child has let you down—denying your values, deciding to live in way you simply can't understand. Or some other loved one has failed you in a serious way.

Whatever it is, nobody asked you. You were not consulted and have no veto power. By no choice of your own, the life you intended to live is over.

What to do? You can try denying reality, or walking away, but the only productive choice you have is to accept the way things are and go from there, doing the best you can. This is the way it was for me, Joseph of Nazareth, a few months ago, on that horrible day when I heard that my dear Mary was pregnant.

Let me back up, start at the beginning. Even though Mary was very young, I wasn't too surprised when her father accepted my offer of marriage. After all, I am of good lineage, descended from Jesse, the father of King David. I'm known not only as a skilled carpenter who makes a comfortable living, but also as a respected citizen and keeper of our Jewish law. A just man. I'm a lot older than Mary, but in our world that is not unusual.

What did surprise me was Mary's happiness in our relationship. This joyous young woman actually seemed enthusiastic about marrying me. It was a miracle! I felt incredibly blessed and went about in a state of euphoria.

In our culture, getting married involves two definite steps. First comes the betrothal ceremony. The groom to be presents the bride's father with a marriage contract and bride price and the couple becomes engaged. For us, an engagement means more than it does for you. It is a formal contract, signifying that the couple is legally married.

After the betrothal, our custom is for the bride to stay with her family for a year or more before the actual marriage ceremony takes place and she moves to her husband's home.

When our trouble began, Mary and I were in the time between these two stages—the betrothal and the marriage. We were committed legally, but had not started living together and consummated the marriage. Down in Judea, the southern part of our country, it was not absolutely forbidden for an engaged couple to make love, but up here in Galilee it is. Here, the rules are very strict. An engaged couple has to wait until the whole marriage process is complete.

Knowing this, you can imagine how I felt on that fateful day when I first heard the gossip, the rumors—"Joseph, Joseph, have you heard?"

I couldn't believe my ears, but when I confronted Mary, my euphoria collapsed into despair. "It is true," she said. "I am with child, but it's not what you think."

Not what I think. What else could I think? What else was there to think?

Then she begged me to listen, and told me some crazy story about God asking her to have this child and sending an angel to speak with her about it. What kind of fool did she think I was?

I stalked out of the room and her house, leaving Mary in tears. I had to get away, to think. What was I to do? Our law is clear. Sexual evil has to be purged from the midst of the people. At worst, justice demanded that Mary be stoned to death by the men of the city for violating my property rights. At the very least, I had to divorce her.

My heart rebelled. I loved Mary. How could I subject her to death, and such a horrible death? How could I even expose her to the disgrace of divorce? I couldn't believe that she was an adulteress—but the evidence was there. Could she have been forced? I just couldn't accept the situation. I struggled for days, miserable and confused.

Then one night I went to bed wondering how to make things as easy as possible for Mary. What would be the quietest, least shameful course of action? I was used to being in charge, to controlling what happened in my life, but now things seemed to be happening to me, limiting my choices, forcing me into actions I didn't want to take.

I lay in bed trying to pray, but all I could do was feel. I felt hurt, anger, betrayal, not only at Mary, but at God. I cried out, "Why me, God? All my life I've played by your rules. I've lived ethically, kept the Sabbath, worshipped in the temple, gone on pilgrimages to Jerusalem for the high holy days. What have I done to deserve this?"

Maybe it was my fault. I should never have asked for Mary. I should have known that someone so gentle and strong, so lovely and good, could never love an ordinary man like me.

Lying there, drenched in pain and self pity, only one thing was clear. I did not want Mary to suffer any more than necessary. Surely God couldn't want that either. It was bad enough for her to go through pregnancy and childbirth in shame. Mercy must temper the law. With that thought in mind I finally fell asleep

Then came the dream. I'd never experienced anything like it. It was a clear message from God just when I needed it. An angel came and spoke to me. "Fear not, Joseph. Don't be afraid to take Mary home. Don't be afraid to marry her." Amazing!

I had thought of mercy, but not to that extent, not to the extent of going through with the marriage. Did God actually want me to keep Mary as my wife?

The angel continued. "The child in Mary's womb is from the Holy Spirit." What? The words made me think of God's Spirit hovering over chaos in the story of creation. If God's Spirit was doing a new act of creation in this child, then sex had absolutely nothing to do with it. That's what Mary had been trying to tell me. Why hadn't I trusted her? Why couldn't I? I knew in my heart that she couldn't, wouldn't, commit adultery.

Then the angel said, "She will bear a son and you will call his name Jesus, for he will save his people from their sins." Yes. The Greek name, Jesus, comes from the Hebrew, Yeshua or Joshua, one who helps or saves. Could it be that this child is the Savior we've been waiting for so many years? The Messiah who would fulfill Isaiah's prophecy and heal creation? And could it be that he is to be both the Son of God most High and Son of David, through me? Was it possible for ordinary people like Mary and me to have a part in God's plan of salvation?

I woke and sat up utterly exalted! Yes, all these questions and wonderings swirled around in my head, but the devastating doubts were gone. Love and faith had managed to overcome fear and suspicion. The huge weight had lifted from my shoulders and my pathway was clear. I would do as the angel said, I would marry Mary and treat the child as my own. It would not be easy. People would gossip, whisper, make ugly comments, but I would not succumb to the temptation of believing them. I would accept and believe my dear wife and the God of my salvation.

And so it was that I went to Mary and her father and asked that we have the marriage ceremony as soon as possible. I wanted to take her home with me where she belonged.

This horrible, wonder-full experience brought me a whole new approach to life. I realized that keeping the law meant more than a life of discipline, prayer and obedience. It meant more than behaving yourself and being in control. In fact, it meant accepting what life hands you, releasing control and living by faith.

Someone said: "To choose what is difficult all one's days, as if it were easy, that is faith," I love that saying and believe it, because it's what I am doing now. Every morning when I get up, I accept the assignment God has given me. I don't ask for another, but embrace it, just as I embrace Mary and this babe she is carrying. God wants me to take care of them, to protect them, and that is what I am doing and will continue to do.

Now it's time for the Roman census, and very soon we must leave for Bethlehem to be counted. I'm concerned about taking Mary—it's so near the time for her to be delivered, but I trust the God who has brought us this far to bring us through that journey too.

Yes. Accepting what life deals out to us is our greatest challenge. Accepting, not with resignation, or dour duty, but with joy and a sense of being graced. Sometimes, what we get doesn't look a bit like a gift. We want to deny it, thrust it aside, demand something different. But you never know. What looks so terrible may not be what it seems. What we think is a calamity, even a tragedy, may turn out to be a blessing—part of God's good plan for us.

Of course some calamities are calamities, with no obvious redeeming qualities, but more often than not, if we're willing to accept what life gives us in a spirit of faith and hope we will find that it's not all negative.

When we know the whole story, painful though it may be, when we can accept reality and look at it in the face—we can start out freshly and honestly, working on whatever new assignment God has given us.

I know my personal assignment, but I don't know yours. Maybe your challenge is to relate to children who have rejected your values, or to give up a relationship you have always treasured.

Maybe you're being asked to take on a responsibility you never asked for or to live with a physical problem that insists on limiting you, keeping you from doing the things you love, things you've always done.

Or perhaps you have a hard time accepting all the new ideas and different people that keep infiltrating into your family, community and world. You'd rather keep things the way they used to be, to bring back the "good old days."

Whatever challenge you face, once you stop struggling and move past the worst of the pain, once you accept the things that cannot be changed, you may find yourself growing and living more deeply and fully than you ever dreamed. You might even uncover new opportunities and exciting insights you've never noticed before. Like me, you may find wonder and joy in something you first saw as anything but a good gift.

Dear friends, I urge you to try to accept your life as God's good gift, just as it is. Take your life in your arms and trust God to guide you in living it out and making it more whole. In the name of Jesus, your Savior and mine.

3

THE ROCK

(The Gospels, passim)

The sea of Galilee is quiet today, with dull blue sky stretching over its waters. I am sitting on the beach, gazing across toward the western hills. Remembering....

My name is Simon, but most of my life I've been called Peter. I am an old man now, and I want to tell you about my long faith journey in several pictures—as a fisherman, as a disciple of Jesus, as a denier of him and as a forgiven follower of the Risen Christ.

First, picture me as a fisherman—busy mending nets, throwing them out into the sea, hauling them in day after day. I grow up catching fish, learning at my father's knee. As a young man I live in Capernaum with my wife, her mother and my brother Andrew. He and I are in the business together with James and John, the sons of our neighbor, Zebedee.

Life seems good, not exciting, but good. The catch isn't always big, but I know that tomorrow will be pretty much the same as today, and rest in that security.

Then one day everything changes. A soft breeze is wafting over the sea of Galilee as I work with Andrew, casting our nets. I am concentrating so hard that I don't even notice a stranger approaching until I hear his voice. Without a word of introduction, he declares, "So you are Simon, son of John. From now on I will call you Cephas." Cephas is Aramaic for Peter, which in turn is the Greek word for rock. (Mark 1:16-20)

And changing my name isn't all this man has in mind. He wants me to change my work too. "Follow me," he says, "and I will make you fish for people."

Later, I find out that the man is Jesus of Nazareth, but at that first moment on the beach I have no idea who he is. Still, there is something compelling about him. His call holds an authority I can not resist. I glance across at Andrew, and immediately we drop our nets and follow him. Then the man approaches James and John, who are mending their nets beside the sea. They too, listen to him and then stop their work immediately. We all leave our nets and boats, our homes and families, and follow him. We just know we have to, but we don't know why, then.

In the second picture I am a disciple, traveling with Jesus and his other followers. In the beginning, there are twelve of us, though later others come along. There are even a few women who travel with us. They support and help with Jesus' ministry of teaching and preaching and healing.

I cannot tell you everything we do, all the adventures we have, but every day I learn something new about Jesus, about life, and about myself. He tells wonderful stories and often teaches in riddles and paradoxes.

We spend a lot of time wondering, exactly who is this Jesus?"

One day he asks us what people are saying about his identity and we tell him that some people think he is John the Baptist, or Elijah, or some other prophet returned to life. Then Jesus challenges us. "Who do you say that I am?" We are stunned into silence, but finally I blurt out the words I've often thought, but never dared to speak. After all, saying such things can get you killed for blasphemy.

"You are the Christ, the Son of the Living God." (Matt 16:-15-16)

Jesus' dark, intense eyes bore straight into mine, and he blesses me—later I learn that this is the only beatitude he ever created for an individual. "Blessed are you, Simon son of Jonah! It is God who has revealed this to you." He goes on, "I tell you, you are Peter, and on this rock I will build my church." (Matt 16:17-19)

What does he mean? I don't find out until long afterward. But the strange thing is that after he makes this amazing statement, he puts his finger to his lips and orders us not to tell anyone that he is the Messiah.

That time Jesus praises me, but a few days later it is a different story. He has started speaking to us in a mysterious and frightening way, telling us that he is going to have to suffer and die in Jerusalem. We know the powers hate him—both the civil and religious authorities are out to get him, but this is too much. I exclaim, "God forbid it, Lord! This must not happen to you."

He turns on me and says sharply, "Get behind me, Satan! You're a stumbling block to me—you're not set on divine things, but human." I am only trying to help, but he is furious.

Then he continues, saying to all of us, "If you want to follow me you must deny yourself, take up your cross and follow me. For those who want to save their life will lose it, and those who lose their life for my sake will find it." Another of his riddles, his paradoxes. (Matt. 16:21-25)

Now it is time to paint the third picture, the one which tells the story of my greatest shame. It is so hard to make myself remember it—to think about it. We have arrived in Jerusalem for the last time. It is Passover, and we sit in an upper room, eating our last meal together.

After dinner we go out to the Mt. of Olives, and Jesus says, "You all will desert me."

In my usual macho style I protest, "Even if everyone deserts you, I will not."

Jesus turns to me with a sad look and says, "This very night, before the cock crows twice, you will deny me three times."

I am aghast—and offended too—how can he say such a thing after all our time together. I answer stoutly, "Even if I must die with you, I will not deny you." Famous last words, last terrible words. (Mark 14:26-31)

Then we go to a garden called Gethsemane, because Jesus wants a quiet place to pray. We can tell he is suffering great stress and needs support when he asks us to watch with him. We start out with good intentions, but fail him when our heads start nodding and we fall asleep. He awakens us with the words "Can you not watch with me one hour?" and goes away to pray some more. The third time he comes back to waken us he says, "Come, let us be going. My betrayer is at hand."

Sure enough, here comes Judas, leading a bunch of armed soldiers. He strides straight up to Jesus and betrays him with a kiss. And what do I do, what do we all do? We desert him and flee. (Matthew 26:36-56)

Later, I skulk into the courtyard, outside the place where they have taken Jesus. I am sitting quietly, waiting to hear what is happening when a servant girl comes up and speaks to me. "You were with Jesus, the Galilean."

"I don't know what you're talking about."

I walk away and go out to the porch. Another servant girl sees me and says to the people standing around, "This man was with Jesus of Nazareth."

I curse, and deny it. "I do not know the man."

After awhile, some bystanders point to me and say, "You are certainly one of them. We can tell by your Galilean accent."

I curse again and declare, "I do not know the man!"

At that moment the cock crows, and I remember what Jesus said to me at dinner. I leave the courtyard, bow my head and weep bitterly. How can Jesus ever have thought I am like a rock—steady and firm. Why did he think that he could count on me? I can't even stick by him when he is in trouble. (Matthew 26:69-75)

The last picture I want you to see is painted after all the terrifying events of Jesus' passion and death and the joy of Easter morning. Some of the other disciples and I are gathered on the beach by the Sea of Galilee late in the evening. We are at loose ends, not knowing what to do with ourselves and feeling kind of low. Resorting to the familiar, I say to them, "I'm going fishing." They all spring to their feet and want to come along.

We spend the whole night in our boat catching absolutely nothing. At daybreak, a man comes and stands on the beach, but we don't realize that he is the Risen Christ. He calls to us, "You don't have any fish, do you?"

"No."

"Throw the net out to the right side of the boat, and you'll find some." We do, and suddenly there are so many fish we can scarcely handle the net.

Then John says, "It is the Lord!" I am so excited that I dive into the sea and start swimming to shore while the rest pull in the net. By the time we all arrive on the beach, Jesus has a charcoal fire burning and asks us to bring him some of the fish we've just caught. Soon he is giving us bread to eat with the fresh fish he's cooked. It is the most delicious breakfast I've ever tasted!

After breakfast, Jesus asks me to come away from the others and sit down beside him on a rock. He asks me, using my old name, "Simon bar John, do you love me more than these?"

"Yes, Lord, you know I love you.

He says, "Feed my lambs." Then he speaks again, "Simon, son of John, do you love me?"

"Yes, Lord, you know I love you."

"Tend my sheep." He asks a third time, "Simon, son of John, do you love me?"

I feel hurt that he keeps asking me the same question, but I answer, "Lord, you know everything, you know that I love you."

Jesus says, "Feed my sheep. And follow me." (John 21:1-19)

We continue sitting there quietly. I think about the question he repeated three times and what he's asking me to do—feed my lambs, tend my sheep, feed my sheep. I remember that long ago he had said that his church, his community, would rest on me. Amazingly, he is repeating that call, still trusting me in spite of the way I denied him. And just as I denied him three times, he is calling me three times, to be his shepherd and care for his people. I am forgiven, accepted and charged with a mission. He still wants me to follow him and serve.

Now, as I sit on this familiar beach remembering his first call to me, the ministry we did together, my shameful denial and his generous grace, I give thanks for the steadfast mercy and kindness of God that I experience through Jesus.

I don't know if you have ever failed or fallen, or made some terrible mistake, but if you have, I declare to you today that God will not give up on you. You can trust God's marvelous love that picks us up, brushes us off and embraces us every time we fall! How amazing to think that we can miss the mark, mess it up or even totally blow it, and still have a second chance—even a third and a fourth or more! Praise be to God!

4

FORGIVEN

(Based on Luke 7:36-50, Romans 5:6-8, and Ephesians 4:32)

I'll never forget that day in Galilee when I dared to enter the house of Simon the Pharisee. Pharisees are Jewish religious leaders we call the separated ones. They keep the law carefully, washing their hands incessantly and avoiding contact with anyone the system labels unclean. For instance, they don't hob nob with shepherds, because their work keeps their hands dirty. And of course they avoid anyone who flouts or breaks the law. That means me. They call me a woman of the streets. Never mind the fact that in our society a woman without the protection of a man has little choice between prostitution and starvation.

You probably know that all women are second class citizens in our world. Between menstruating and child bearing, we spend a good part of our lives labeled unclean. As a prostitute I am considered unclean all the time--someone to be avoided and excluded. But I've heard Jesus teaching, and watched him speak to women with the same attention and respect as men. He even shares table fellowship with people like me, prostitutes and sinners. Once I was part of a group that sat down to eat with him. He made me feel forgiven, acceptable for the first time in years. I longed to let him know how grateful I am.

The Pharisees are careful never to sit down at table with the wrong kind of people, so the day Simon invited Jesus to eat at his house, the other guests were carefully selected—Pharisees and other upstanding citizens. I really don't understand why Simon has included Jesus, since he is known to eat with prostitutes and other unsavory types. Maybe Simon wants to test him, or just enjoys collecting celebrities.

In warm weather, people often set meals with a visiting rabbi out in the courtyard so uninvited townspeople can come in, listen to the table conversation and hear the teacher's wise answers. Others can come, but of course not people like me. I know this. I know I am breaking the rules and will likely get in trouble, but I have to see Jesus and thank him for making me feel like a human being again. I cross the street and peer into Simon's shady courtyard. In the center is a flowing fountain, inviting and cool on that sweltering day. I slip inside, quietly and quickly, and approach the table were the guests are gathered.

When I arrive the guests are already seated according to our custom, reclining on low couches around the table. They lean back on their left elbow, leaving the right arm and hand free for eating. Their feet are extended behind them.

I walk over and stand by Jesus' feet. He turns and smiles when he sees me. When our eyes meet, my heart overflows, along with my tears. Sinking to my knees behind him, I take the alabaster vial of sweet smelling ointment I always wear around my neck, uncork it, and begin to anoint him. My tears are dampening his feet, and I have no towel to dry them. What to do? Even though I know perfectly well that no respectable woman ever loosens her hair in public, I unbind mine, wipe off his feet, and kiss them.

Simon notices what I am doing and reproves Jesus, "Disgusting! How can you let that woman touch you? If you are a true prophet you should know what kind of woman she is—a sinner."

But Jesus speaks up and says, "Simon, I have something to say to you."

"Speak, teacher," Simon growls.

Then Jesus tells a story, "A certain creditor had two debtors; one owed him five hundred denarii and the other owed fifty." (In case you don't know, a denarius is an average day's wage.) "It turned out that neither one could pay, and much to their surprise, the creditor forgave both debts. Now, which one do you think will love the creditor more?"

"I suppose the one whose debt is greater," Simon answered.

"You're right," said Jesus. He turned toward me and then said to Simon, "Look at this woman. When I entered your house you did not offer me basic hospitality. You did not give me water for my feet, but she bathed my feet with her tears and dried them with her hair. You did not give me a welcoming kiss, but she has not stopped kissing my feet. You did not anoint my head with oil but she has anointed me with fragrant ointment. And I tell you, the great love she has shown proves that her sins, which were many, have been forgiven. But whoever has been forgiven little shows only a little love."

Then Jesus says to me, "Your sins are forgiven. Go in peace."

"Thank you, teacher," I whisper to Jesus as I start to leave. Then I look around at the other guests and hear them saying to one another, "Who is this who even forgives sins?"

But I, I have experienced it and know it is true. Jesus can forgive sins; he has forgiven the sin that has bound me tightly for so many years. It is all I can do to keep from shouting "I am forgiven!" as I walk proudly out of Simon's courtyard into the sunlight, healed and free.

*   *   *   *   *

All through scripture, judgment and forgiveness are two sides of the same coin, two dimensions of God's healing activity. But in Christ, and his work on the cross, God bears the cost of our waywardness and sin, freely offering us the acceptance and forgiveness we can never deserve or earn. Our job is to receive it and make it part of our lives.

How do we do this?

First we must know and feel our need, like the woman in the story. We must realize we need forgiving. If we go around saying, "There's nothing wrong with me. I'm certainly not as bad as that guy over there," Haven't you known people like that, who always think they're fine—it's the other person who has a problem? If we don't think we need it, that we're OK as is, we can't and we won't experience God's forgiveness.

I know it's not very fashionable to talk about feeling sinful, that we're supposed to give up guilt and develop self-esteem, but I think the great psychiatrist, Carl Jung, was probably right in thinking that guilt was the root of every problem people brought to him. If we have insight and sensitivity, some sense of guilt is healthy. That's why it's important to offer prayers of confession, recognizing our tendency to do the things we ought not to have done and failure to do the things we ought to have done. This is a realistic attitude, a matter of being honest, not wallowing in negativity.

Jesus said that no one, including himself, is good but God alone. As Christians we need to recognize that we all fall short before God. Our human nature is a mixed bag of good and evil. We're made in God's image, yes, but that image is tarnished by alienation and self-seeking. We are vulnerable and subject to temptation. Or to put it in traditional language, we are all sinners.

We can see this problem in our habit of putting the best light on ourselves and what we do. Consider the husband and wife who had the habit of tossing their clothes toward the laundry hamper each night. In the morning one of them picked up the items that missed and put them in. One day the wife was feeling put upon and said to her husband, "I wish that you would take more responsibility for picking up the clothes that miss the hamper."

Thinking that he already did about 75% of the picking up, he asked her, "How often do you think you do it?."

"Oh," she answered, "about 75% of the time.

I think the second step toward receiving forgiveness is like one of the twelve steps in Alcoholics Anonymous. We need to admit our helplessness to help ourselves and look to a higher power. Salvation, being in right relationship with God and others, is not a do it yourself project, despite what the self-help books say.

I believe that it was this insight that converted me to Christian faith. Everyone comes to faith differently, and you may not relate to my experience---but I want to tell you about my conversion. Back when I was in college I took a course in the life and teachings of St. Paul When we read Romans, his teaching about human nature was a revelation to me. His words are complicated and sometimes confusing, but a couple of verses came through to me with clarity and power. He says "I can will what is right, but I cannot do it, For I do not do the good I want, but the evil I do not want is what I do." (Romans 7:18b-19) To me, this is a profound expression of psychological reality.

My early idea of being a Christian was to be and do good. I had always thought that people are basically good and that education is the answer to human evil. If we know what is right, we will do it. But as I experienced more of people and the world I saw that this isn't true. Often we know the right thing and really want to do it, but don't follow through. We are a mixed bag of good and evil and need help from outside ourselves to be the people we want to be.

It was this new sense that the power of sin keeps us from living the good lives we intend, that converted me to an understanding of Christian faith as the interaction of God's gracious forgiveness and our response. Gradually, I came to the place where I understood that I could never earn forgiveness, or make myself into the kind of person I wanted to be all by myself. I knew I needed to ask God for help in beginning a new kind of life.

Once we recognize our need for forgiveness, the third step is turning toward God in faith, trusting that God will forgive and receive us just as we are. We don't have to shape up first. Folk tradition lifts up this same theme of transformation through acceptance. Think of the story of Beauty and the Beast. The Beast is still ugly and fearsome when Beauty commits herself to staying with him. It is her love and acceptance that transform him back into a handsome prince.

It is the same in our faith story. As St. Paul puts it in another part of Romans, "While we were yet sinners, Christ died for us."(5:8) And in the story we just heard, Jesus forgives and accepts the woman before she decides to turn her life around, not afterward. Her expression of love is the result, not the cause, of her being forgiven. Her gratitude overflows when she receives forgiveness.

Fourth, and last, we need to forgive ourselves. The great theologian Paul Tillich proclaims "You are accepted. All you have to do is accept the fact you are accepted." We could adapt this to read, "You are forgiven. All you have to do is accept the fact you are forgiven."

"All you have to do"--it sounds easy, but for many of us it's anything but. Unlike those who think they do better than others and don't need forgiving, some of us are hard on ourselves and struggle with endless guilt. We feel responsible in situations where we are not at fault. And we can't forgive ourselves when we do something wrong or remember a past mistake. We torture ourselves—why did I say this, why did I do this? Or why didn't I?

A lot of us are caught in a sort of perfectionism, thinking we should always do everything right. When we take on too much responsibility, we need to think of the words of a sign I keep on my computer printer. It is a letter from God which reads: "Do not feel totally, personally, irrevocably, responsible for everything. That's my job. Signed, God."

So let's cut ourselves some slack. Let's try to stop adding up our defects and failings, and allow ourselves to accept God's acceptance. If God, who is perfect, can forgive us, maybe we can begin to forgive ourselves.

These four steps allow us to receive God's gracious forgiveness: knowing our need, realizing we need help, turning to God in faith, and forgiving ourselves. But the journey into forgiveness does not end there. God calls us to respond to the gift of forgiveness by forgiving others.

The Amish people believe that forgiveness is the central healing reality and responsibility of their faith. When a gunman entered a classroom in Nickel Mine, Pennsylvania, and killed five of their daughters, wounded five others and then killed himself, they refused to balance hurt with hate. Amid their own loss and grief they reached out to the shooter's stricken family in forgiveness and support.

To me, the Amish spirit stands as a challenge to us who think of ourselves as recipients of God's grace. Forgiveness has the power to transform both forgiver and the forgiven. Our sense of being loved and forgiven enables us to follow Paul's teaching in Ephesians and "be kind, tenderhearted, forgiving one another as God in Christ has forgiven you." May it be so.

5

WHO TOUCHED ME?

(Based on Mark 5:21-43)

Twelve years—my blood had been flowing for twelve long years. Day and night, I had coped with the discomfort and embarrassment of the problem. I'd gone to every doctor I could find, spent all my money.

The doctors put me through some imaginative cures, but the hemorrhaging got worse, not better. Finally they just threw up their hands, "Nothing can be done, woman. Just learn to live with your problem."

Did they have any idea what they were saying? Accepting my problem meant being uncomfortable, tired and listless every day for the rest of my life. It was draining to lose all that blood! But the physical side wasn't the worst of it. Worst of all was the loneliness. If I couldn't be healed I always would be isolated, cut off from other people. Why? Because our Jewish law in Leviticus pronounces that menstruating women are unclean, not only during their period, but for a whole week afterward. Women are also unclean after childbirth, for 7 days after the birth of a boy, plus 33 days of purification. The time doubles for a baby girl,14 days of uncleanness and 66 days of purification. You can imagine how welcome baby girls were. For a mother it meant 80 days of restriction. No wonder everyone wanted boys.

On top of all that, a new mother has to make a sin offering at the end of her purification. A SIN offering! How strange! In our world we value women primarily for bearing children, but when they do what they are supposed to do, they have to pay a penalty. It isn't easy being a woman in our time and place. It comes naturally to feel you're not worth much, even that you're filthy.

In my case, the continual flow of blood made me perpetually unclean. I had to stay out of polite society, away from people. I only went out to see doctors or to get food and other supplies. And I made it a point to go when few people were around. If I did meet anyone, I kept my distance so I wouldn't brush against them by mistake.

Oh yes, I forgot to tell you that being unclean makes you dangerous because uncleanness is contagious. Anything or anyone you touch becomes unclean too. Men are especially vulnerable. If you come near them they are supposed to shout "Begone, you filthy woman!" Then you have to get gone fast, or take the consequences.

Along with all the doctors, I've tried home remedies and faith healers. I've even tried prayer, though I doubted that God would hear me. After all, everyone knows that trouble and illness come direct from God. Our religion teaches that poor health shows God's anger or disfavor. My incurable ailment meant that God was punishing me for something I'd done wrong. The trouble is I don't know what.

Some days I felt like giving up and just accepting my situation, but rebellious feelings lurked around the edges of my mind. There must be a way. I had to be healed!

Late one day when the crowds had thinned, I was in town buying supplies, and heard some people talking about a healer from Nazareth, Jesus, by name.

An old man said, "He has driven out evil spirits and healed many diseases."

"Yes," said another, "but he's in trouble with the Pharisees and religious leaders for healing on the Sabbath and eating with prostitutes and sinners."

"I don't care. He'll be here tomorrow and I for one want to see him."

Now I was skeptical of faith healers, so many were phony, but this man sounded different. Maybe he could see beyond the rules of the pollution system to the yearnings of the heart. Maybe he would care about the need of an unclean woman like me. Even his name means, "He saves."

Hope flickered in my heart and I resolved to go and see for myself. I would dare to try for healing one more time. I would take the risk.

And it would be a risk. First, it meant going out in a crowd, mixing with people. Worse, it meant approaching a male religious teacher in all my uncleanness. Why would he help the likes of me? What would they do to me if I was caught? I almost talked myself out of the idea, but finally I decided to go and see Jesus. I had to try.

The next morning dawned bright, beautiful and warm, but I bundled up just the same and put on my heaviest veil. I didn't want to be recognized and sent home before I even saw Jesus.

I walked with my head down, trying to be as inconspicuous as possible. When I neared the center of town I heard a commotion and saw a great crowd gathered around Jairus, a leader of the synagogue, and a man I'd never seen before. The stranger must be Jesus. They were talking intently, and as I grew closer I heard Jairus begging Jesus, "Please. Please come and heal my daughter—she's at the point of death."

Jesus agreed, and they began to move away, as fast as they could in that mob of people. O no! After struggling to gather my courage and come here, was I going to miss meeting the healer? Somehow I knew that he was the one I'd been looking for, that his power would heal me. I must not lose this chance. I would catch up with them and at least touch the hem of his robe. Even that might heal me.

I pushed my way through the crowd, not worrying about how many people I touched. Some gave me unfriendly looks, but thank heaven no one recognized me. At last I was right behind Jesus and I reached out, tentatively. Then I dared to reach decisively and touch the fringe of his garment, very quickly, very lightly.

As I made contact I felt the flow of blood stop, just like that. After 12 long years it actually stopped.

Before I could leap for joy and praise God, I froze in fear and trembling, for Jesus had stopped in his tracks. He stood stock still and asked, "Who touched me?" Then he looked all around.

His disciples thought it was a strange question. After all, in that crowd everyone was touching and jostling each other. But Jesus knew the difference between jostling and intentional touching. He also knew that he had released power, and I knew I had to confess.

Hanging my head, I slunk up to him. At one level I was terrified, but at another, I was angry and thought, "How crazy is it to live in a world where you have to apologize for wanting to be healed? Would he be angry? Would he say, "Be gone, woman," or worse?"

I fell on my knees before him and he looked down at me. Slowly, I raised my eyes to his. His face was not angry, but gentle and strong and filled with intense concern. Something in his look released all my dammed up feelings. I poured out my story—what it was like for me, the discomfort, the loneliness, the inability to have a life. I can't describe how wonderful it felt to be with Jesus, to talk, and know he was listening.

Then he spoke with the most profound compassion. Not, "Woman, begone," but "Daughter, your faith has made you whole. Go in peace"

He had healed me of that bloody scourge and now he was wishing me shalom, peace and well being under God. I wondered if he knew what he was doing in being so good to me. Did he realize the risk he was taking in defying the blood taboo?

You could say that my healing had two dimensions. First came the physical, the end of the bleeding, and then the personal, the encounter with Jesus and his word of acceptance and salvation. He even called me "daughter." To him I was just as much a daughter of the faith as Jairus' little girl.

But what about her? I had interrupted Jesus on his way to help that child. Just then something horrible happened. People from Jairus' household came rushing up to him, crying, "Your daughter is dead!" Was it my fault for delaying Jesus? Did my healing come at the cost of the little girl's life? I couldn't bear the thought.

The men were saying to Jairus, "It's over, don't trouble the teacher any longer." They were sure there was no use, it was time for Jairus to give up hope.

But Jesus would not do any such thing. He said to Jairus, "Do not be afraid, only believe." Gesturing to four of his disciples to follow them, he gave me a quick smile and strode off toward Jairus' house.

For a moment I stood there, frozen, but I had to know what happened. I crept along behind them, far enough back to be un-noticed. Jesus entered Jairus' house and sent out all the wailing relatives except for the girl's father and mother.

A little later Jairus and his wife came out of the house, smiling. I heard them say that everyone had mocked Jesus when he entered and said the girl was only sleeping, but he paid no attention and sent them away. Then he took the little girl's hand and said, *Talitha cum*, which means "Little girl, get up," raising her from the sleep of death. She got up immediately and started walking around. Then Jesus told them to give her something to eat.

Marvelous! Now at last I could rejoice in the gifts of my healing and hers!

Looking back at that amazing day---the day my life began again—I couldn't help thinking that Jairus and I weren't all that different—he, a ruler of the synagogue and I, an unclean woman.

> Both of us were desperate, unwilling to make peace with our misery.
> Both of us refused to let go of hope. We trusted beyond reason.
> Both of us dared to reach out for healing, knowing and taking the risks involved. Jairus defied other Jewish leaders who hated and feared Jesus. I dared to defy the pollution system that labeled me worthless and unclean.
> Jairus could have accepted his daughter's illness and death as God's will.
> I could have resigned myself to life-long misery and loneliness.
> We could have "bought into" the teaching that told us we must have done something wrong to deserve our troubles.
> We could have, but we did not.

Instead, Jairus and I dared to reach out to a healer who refused to abide by all the rules and labels. We dared to turn to the Jesus who knew that God's will for everyone is for health, wholeness and abundant life. When we reached out, our faith and the power of God in Jesus came together with force and healing happened. Praise be to God!

And there's more. The very same day I was healed from my bleeding and isolation, I was cured of my own fear and judgmentalism and opened to a new spirit of empathy and compassion. I had always hated and feared Jairus and his kind. After all, they were the ones who condemned me to a life of loneliness. But on that great day, I saw that Jairus, with all his power, was just as needy as I, just as needy.

Since then, I have come to believe that every single one of us, every member of the human family, has a burden to bear—large or small, light or heavy. I have been drawn out of my own troubles into relationship with others who also have pain to conquer and rough roads to travel. Struggles, problems, and hurts afflict us all, and we all need the touch of the Healer.

Dear friends, I don't know all the burdens you are carrying today, what pains, problems, or long sorrow you are bearing, but whatever your burden, I do know you do not have to accept it as inevitable and give in to its weight. You don't have to give in or give up. You have a choice. You may never be cured, but you can be healed. You can turn to your Savior God, who heals and redeems your life. You can wallow in your pain or reach out to Jesus for healing and be whole. May it be so!

6

AT LEAST THE CRUMBS

(Based on Mark 7:24-30, Matthew 15:21-28)

How is it with you today? Are you feeling good—or have you come here with a sense of need? Hungry for healing, for hope?

I have come to speak with you of food that will satisfy your hunger—not just junk food, but the real thing. Nourishing food, the Bread of Life, for you and for everyone.

I am Anna, a Syro-Phoenician woman, a Canaanite, from the district around Tyre and Sidon. As a true daughter of Canaan, I have always despised the Jews. After all, they're descendants of the Israelite invaders who drove my people out of the land because they said God promised it to them. They hate us Gentiles too, and look down on our religion. They cannot see the beauty of our faith, with its emphasis on birth, growth, death and rebirth, the eternal cycle of nature. They call us pagans, unclean, no better than street dogs.

Now, under the Roman occupation, Jewish arrogance is worse, even insufferable. They believe that only they are acceptable to God. And those Pharisees, their holier than thou religious leaders, think that they are so superior. They teach that any contact with Gentiles will soil them. In Jewish eyes, we are utterly unacceptable, outcasts, just because we're different, foreign, not like them. What self-respecting Gentile would want contact with such bigots? Who would want to talk with or even go near those racist Jews? We're glad to stay away from them.

But let me tell you what happened to me a couple of weeks ago, why I changed my mind and talked with a Jew. Yes, and more—I actually knelt down before a Jewish man and poured out my heart before him.

I have a daughter, little Leah, just trembling on the edge of womanhood. She is so dear, yet so afflicted. In childhood, a powerful demon began coming upon her unexpectedly, knocking her down. She stiffened, and was seized with convulsions. Her sweet face contorted into a horrible grimace and often I feared she would swallow her tongue. Then she would lose consciousness. It was horrifying!

How Leah suffered, and how I suffered with her, for her. I hated that demon and longed to see it driven out of her body, her life. But it was not to be. As she grew older, the attacks grew more frequent and more severe. How could she live a normal life, marry, have children? Would she be able to live at all—or would that demon kill her?

I tried every remedy suggested by our healers, but nothing worked. I prayed and prayed to our ancient gods and made rich sacrifices to them, but still the demon kept on coming. It seemed to be laughing at us and our efforts. Bit by bit I began to wonder about the power of our gods. Were they real gods, or only images, statues? I longed for the help of a God who was strong and able. I needed a healer who was more powerful than that malignant demon, more powerful than nature. But I knew of no such God or healer, and grew nearer and nearer despair.

One day, I heard about a healer who worked beyond our borders. He was a Jew, a traveling Rabbi named Jesus, who was preaching and healing in Galilee. I kept hearing stories about him. He could make the lame walk and the blind see. And yes, he could drive out evil demons and heal the people they attacked. The stories were amazing, but they weren't all I heard. There was more. People said this Jesus was kind and compassionate. He cared for the *anawim*, the people of the land—the little people—not just the rich and powerful, not just the religious and pure. In fact, the very religious people like the Pharisees didn't like him at all and disapproved of his work. They condemned him because he ate with prostitutes and sinners, even tax collectors! What manner of man could this be? I heard that Jesus even talked to women and treated them with dignity. Best of all, and how my ears pricked up at this, he loved children. Instead of shooing them away like most religious leaders, he called them to him and set them on his knee! He even told his followers that they needed to become like children—humble and open—to enter the Kingdom of God.

I began to plan. I would travel to Galilee and find this Jesus. I would beg him to heal my Leah. Deep down, I knew that he could help us—that he was the one who carried God's healing power within him. But then, more news traveled to me. I heard that Jesus had left Galilee and was traveling our way, into Tyre and Sidon, the district not far from my home. Surely it was a sign!

I arranged for a friend to stay with my daughter and hurried to the place where Jesus and his followers were staying. I saw them from a distance, a motley crew, even including a few women. They were gathering up their belongings, and it looked as if they were getting ready to set out on the road again. There, standing to one side of the group, was Jesus. It had to be Jesus—everyone's attention was focused on him, waiting for his word, his signal to depart.

I was still far away, and they were leaving. Oh, I mustn't miss Jesus. I must get his attention. I picked up my pace and cried out from a distance. "Have mercy upon me, O Lord, Son of David. My daughter is severely possessed by a demon. Have mercy!"

Did he hear me? He did not answer.

I hurried nearer, crying out my need again and again. His disciples heard me all right. They turned and looked at me with ugly stares. I heard a couple of them say to Jesus, "Send that Canaanite woman away. She keeps crying after us." Were these the followers of the Rabbi who was said to be so kind and compassionate? How could their hearts be so hard?

But I was in for a still greater shock. By then I had reached Jesus and bowing down respectfully, I said, "Help me, Lord."

He turned and looked at me with deep dark eyes and said gently, "I was sent only to the lost sheep of the house of Israel."

What did he mean? Was he saying that he would not help me—that he only ministered to Jews—that no Gentiles need apply? Was he like all the rest? I could not, I would not, accept it. I had to show him how much I needed him, how much I trusted him to help me.

I knelt down before Jesus. I could feel strength and power exuding from his being. Surely he was of God. I felt overwhelmed. My carefully thought out words, my argument would not come. All I could say was "Lord, help me, my daughter is so very ill."

Jesus answered, still gently, but firmly, "Let the children be fed first, for it is not fair to take the children's food and throw it to the dogs." Dogs! How could Jesus use that cruel term for another human being? Was he just like the Pharisees who think they are so superior, and we Gentiles, so worthless? I couldn't believe he was like that. And besides he hadn't used the word they usually use to insult us, the word for a street dog, a mangy scavenger. No. Jesus had used the word for a little dog, a family pet. Maybe he spoke as he did for his disciples' benefit—to show them how narrow their traditional language and attitudes sounded. Or maybe he was probing my heart, testing to see if I truly trusted him and had confidence in his power. I didn't know.

But then again, maybe it didn't matter. Perhaps it was best to give up trying to break through the barrier between us. Who was I, a Gentile and a woman, to dare to talk back to this important rabbi? I probably was offending him just by asking for help. But this was no moment for caution. I couldn't give up. My daughter's life hung in the balance. This was my only chance, he was my only hope. What did I have to lose?"

But what more could I say? What would convince this wise rabbi of my faith, my trust in his healing power? My mind raced—considering his words: "It is not fair to give the children's food to the dogs."

I thought of a familiar scene at our dinner table. We don't have napkins the way you do. Instead, we use little pieces of bread for napkins—wiping our fingers and then dropping the bread on the floor. I thought of how our family dogs wait patiently for those morsels to fall and then scramble to gobble them up.

Words came to me. "Yes, Lord, yet even the dogs under the table eat the children's crumbs."

Jesus gazed at me for a long moment with those deep, dark eyes. Then he smiled slowly. Such a magnificent, generous smile! He raised his hand in a sign of blessing and said, "Woman, great is your faith. For saying that, you may go—the demon has left your daughter."

I stood and thanked him profusely. Then I rushed home and found Leah completely healed. The demon had departed never to come again. My daughter was saved from a life of torment and sorrow. She could live in peace—a normal life. She is living a normal life!

To the end of my days I will praise and thank my Lord Jesus who broke through the towering barriers of our world to heal my daughter and feed her on the Bread of Life. I will follow him and his way, refusing to limit my loving to my own kind, my own people. What about you? Aren't you his followers too? Today, ask yourself, "Do I build walls between myself and other people, or do I do my best to tear them down? Do I insulate myself from people who seem different, distasteful or unacceptable? Or do I refuse to let cruel barriers divide me from others? Do I reach out to accept and receive everyone in the name of the Lord Jesus who loves us all and comes bringing the Bread of Life for everyone?

7

UNBENDING

(Based on Luke 13:10-17)

I open my eyes slowly, awakening to another dreary day of looking at feet instead of faces. Today is the Sabbath, and I want to worship, so I bestir myself to get up, moving slowly, as always. It isn't easy to get my ungainly, bent body out of bed. Finally standing, at least part way, I gather my clothes and start the struggle to put them on. Then I eat a bite of bread, washed down with a swallow of water from the jug on my table and head out the door.

It is exhausting to live bent over, almost double, and I've been that way for 18 years. Think of it. If you've ever bent over to pick something up only to find yourself unable to stand up again—if you've ever had your back go out on you, or it has been painful, aching or stiff—you have some inkling of what my back feels like every single day.

And that's just the physical side. My condition stands in the way of normal relationships. Being bent over means that I stare at the ground. I'm unable to see straight ahead, to look people in the eyes. No-one wants to look at an unsightly cripple either, so my stooped posture separates me from others and makes me isolated and lonely.

All women have low status in our world. The rabbis love to say things like, "woe to those whose children are daughters," and "the woman is in all things inferior to the man." With an infirmity like mine, and no husband or son or other protector, I am not just inferior, but worth less than nothing. I have gone to countless doctors and healers, but no one has been able to help. Some people say that Satan had bound me this way, but others think that God is punishing me. Surely only someone who has committed a terrible sin would be bent over for 18 years. Either way, I am an outcast, even though I have always done my best to be an observant and faithful Jewish woman.

Slowly, I make my way to the synagogue. The feet of many people are gathered in the courtyard, more than usual. There is a sense of excitement in the air, and I crane my neck to try to see what is going on. For me it is easier to see from a distance, and across the courtyard I glimpse an unfamiliar rabbi teaching the people. They are listening eagerly, but some Pharisees and the officers of the synagogue hover around the edges of the crowd, looking less than pleased.

As I stand there, straining to hear what the rabbi is saying, his voice pauses and stops. Of course, I can't see very well, but I seem to feel the rabbi's gaze resting on me. I hate being noticed, and freeze where I am, frightened. Are those his feet walking toward me? Is he on his way to lecture me? To condemn me or use me as a terrible example?

After a moment, I am sure the sandaled feet are coming closer. Then they stop right in front of me. I feel a hand resting gently on my head and hear the rabbi's voice speaking. "Woman, you are freed from your infirmity. You are free." Can it be?

It is unbelievable. I feel a loosening in my back, and a creaking as vertebrae by vertebrae I raise myself to my full height. Then I am standing straight and raise my arms to the heavens in thanksgiving. Hallelujah!

Before I can bow before the rabbi and offer thanks, I hear the harsh voice of the ruler of the synagogue raking over the crowd. "Just look at this law breaker! There are six days, six whole days, when it is legal to heal. Why does he have to choose the seventh day, the holy Sabbath to do this work? It's outrageous!"

The rabbi refuses to accept this kind of abuse and answers, "Hypocrites! You tend your animals on the Sabbath and loosen them from their tethers to give them water. Why in the world shouldn't this woman of faith, this daughter of Abraham, who has been bound by Satan for 18 long years, be loosened and freed from her infirmity on the holy Sabbath?"

Perhaps they feel shame, but the leaders of the synagogue fall silent as the people rejoice with me and give thanks. Praise be to God!

* * * * *

This is one of several Gospel stories about Jesus defying Jewish law to heal on the Sabbath. It is easier to appreciate its meaning and power if you know something about the importance and rigidity of the Sabbath law in Jesus' day.

It was illegal to work on the Sabbath, the day of rest when all good Jews remember and celebrate how God rested from the work of creation. But there were many questions about what constituted work. The rabbis debated the issue endlessly in minute detail. For example, you could not build a fire or cook. Nor could you pick a hair out of your soup if you were lucky enough to have some all ready to eat. On the other hand, you could exercise, feed and water your animals.

Healing was classified as work and the details were clearly defined. Medical help could be given only if a life was in danger. You could assist a woman undergoing a difficult or dangerous labor, but you could not treat a sprain or fracture. You could wrap a cut with a plain bandage to stem the bleeding, but it was illegal to use a healing ointment. The bottom line was that you could act to keep a condition or injury from getting worse or killing someone, but you couldn't try to make it better. It's hard for us to understand this, but that was the law in first century Judaism.

With these beliefs about work in mind, think about the story from the perspective of the ruler of the synagogue. Try to identify with him as the guardian of the faith and God's holy law. He isn't just being arbitrary and mean, but he is a stickler for rules and regulations. He believes that if standards are relaxed for even a moment, or if one exception is made, the whole structure of faith and order may collapse. He has real feelings and concerns about his responsibility in relation to what Jesus is doing. Why in the world can't this visiting rabbi and healer obey the law and be a good role model for the people by healing on any day but the Sabbath? After all, this woman has been bent over for 18 years, what difference does one more day make? To him, Jesus just showing off, setting himself above the law.

Now think of how Jesus sees the situation. He looks out at the crowd and notices everyone and everything—even a disabled woman of no importance. His heart goes out to her. She is bent over painfully, awkwardly, and has been so for very long time. Jesus asks why should this member of the faith, this daughter of Abraham, endure her disability for one moment longer? He sees a suffering person and acts to heal immediately. He cares about the law of his faith, yes, but he does not believe that it should supersede human need or delay healing.

One healing—three perspectives: to the woman it's an amazing and unexpected gift of grace, to the ruler it's an outrageous flouting of the law, and to Jesus, it's an urgent, God directed act of compassion and healing. What is our perspective? How can this story speak to us now?

We can begin by asking some of the ways people are bent over these days, both literally or figuratively. What problems and pressures afflict us and diminish human lives. Heaven knows that women in many parts of the world are still bent low by cultural attitudes and customs, denied education and productive work. I've been reading the book, *Half the Sky*, the title of which is based on the Chinese proverb "Women hold up half the sky." It is painful to read, with its true stories, of daughters sold into sexual slavery to help support the family and honor killings, where women who are raped are killed to purge the family of their polluting presence. In India, women are sometimes murdered to rid the family of the burden of finding dowries to buy them husbands. There, in China, and elsewhere, gender related abortion is still a common practice. Fortunately, along with delineating the problems, the book describes efforts organizations and foundations are making to unbend and improve the lives of these women.

Many members of minorities, people with disabilities, and immigrants feel bent down by the way some see and treat them. And then there is the bending power of difficult childhoods, disappointed dreams, destructive or broken relationships, mental or physical illness. Some of us feel bent by the sheer complexity of life in this complicated and confusing world and the enormity of the decisions we have to make.

I believe that a lot of us are bent over in some way, to some degree, whether by fierce pressures and choices, long sorrow, or deep wounds in our lives. None of us is immune. Sometimes our hurts and anxieties run so deep that we aren't consciously aware of them. Sometimes we pretend they aren't there—covering them over with hard work and bright smiles. Our bentness isn't always as obvious as that of the woman in the story.

Whatever our struggles may be, I often wonder how people manage to stand up straight without faith. We need help from outside ourselves. Jesus offered the woman in the synagogue nothing less than transformation, and that is what he offers us today. Jesus started the process before he placed his healing hands on that woman's head and spoke those great words of liberation. He started it by the simple act of noticing her, of refusing to accept the notion that she was of no account. In that first moment he conferred dignity upon her and her life began to change. Then came touch, that healing touch, and those wonderful words, "Woman, you are freed from your infirmity." After all those years the bent woman stood up straight. I just love picturing her as she slowly rises to the same level with the rest of the people. I imagine her wondering, "Can this really be happening?" finally making eye contact with others, smiling.

No delay," said Jesus, that day in the synagogue. "No delay," says he to us. God wants us to be freed from what ails us right now. God wants you and me to unbend, to throw off everything that cripples or oppresses or wounds us—to stand up straight and be all we are meant to be, not tomorrow, but today. Jesus wants us to turn to him in faith, trusting in his healing power.

And we can help each other unbend, beloved. We can participate in Christ's healing and liberating work. We don't have to be miracle workers, but we do need to notice our neighbors and take thought for their problems. We can open our hands and hearts to help in large and small ways. So often a smile, a touch a simple act of caring can make all the difference. I will never forget the difficult summer before my husband Walter died and the wonderful support we received---real assistance in unbending from family and friends and pastors. People gave their time and encouragement in many ways. Our pastor lent his knowledgeable presence as we searched for a place where Walter could get the care he needed. Ray visited Walter regularly and one day Gail and Vicky came to his room and sang his favorite hymns with us—a wonderful lift! God's healing worked powerfully through all that love.

I want to close with a simple story of unbending. Some pastor friends of ours adopted two Ukrainian boys. After surviving all the waiting and making their way through miles of red tape, they brought the boys to California and they began to adapt to a new home here. It wasn't easy. Both of them arrived bent way down from their deprived and difficult life in the orphanage. One day, their new dad brought them up to Sonora to meet us. They were learning English, but didn't know much yet. The older boy spoke a little, and enjoyed calling everything he liked "cool." He seemed to be doing OK. But the other child was silent and withdrawn. As we sat at the table having a snack, he kept his head down, staring at his cookie instead of us.

Before the family arrived I had put Zoe, our little Welsh Corgi outside. She was still a puppy then and I feared that her bouncy enthusiasm might be too much for the children. Now, I decided it was just what we needed. I brought Zoe in and she made a beeline for the boys. Both of them jumped up from the table and before we knew it they were rolling around on the floor with Zoe having a wonderful time rubbing her tummy and getting their faces thoroughly washed. Now the younger boy lifted his gaze, laughing and smiling. The joyful little dog had managed to unbend him, to help him stand up straighter. If she could do it, with God's help, surely you and I can reach out to release the people we know who need unbending. May it be so.

8

THE WOMAN AT THE WELL

(Based on John 4:5-42, Psalm 42)

INTRODUCTION

This first person story sermon is based on John's story of Jesus and the Samaritan woman at Jacob's well. It's a wonderful story, but complex and full of symbolism, like much of John's Gospel.

In order to understand the woman's story, you need to know that the Judean and Samaritan Jews had despised each other for hundreds of years. They were all Jews, but the Judeans considered the Samaritans not real Jews—corrupt and unclean because they had intermarried with foreigners. Also, the two groups worshipped in different places—the Samaritans at Mt. Gerazim and the Judeans, in Jerusalem. In his conversation with the woman at the well, Jesus announces that the barriers between the two peoples are being demolished.

THE WOMAN AT THE WELL

The sun is already high as I set out from the little Samaritan village of Sychar, near the foot of Mount Gerazim. It's almost noon, the time of day when no one in their right mind even thinks of working outside. My head scarf and dress are loosely woven, rather like the fabric you call burlap, but the relentless sun and the perspiration soaking my back combine to make me feel as though I'm melting. Waves of heat are even radiating up from the ground.

How I wish I could go to draw my water early in the morning or at dusk like the other women—but they don't want me around for their socializing at the well. The fact is I'm an outcast, and offer frequent fodder for their gossip. The respectable women call me immoral because of my history with men. They condemn me because I've had five husbands and am now living with another man. So I have no choice but to go when no one else is at the well. I hoist my bucket onto my head and make my way slowly to Jacob's well. I am alone in every way.

While I walk along, I meditate, saying my favorite psalm to myself. "As the deer pants for flowing streams, so my souls longs for you, O God. My soul thirsts for God, for the living God. When shall I come and behold the face of God. My tears have been my food day and night, while people say to me continually, where is thy God?" That Psalmist knows exactly how I feel.

Jacob's well is a treasured spot among the Jews, and full of memories for them. Jacob bought it on his death bed and bequeathed it to his son, Joseph, who is buried there. Sad to say, Jews and Samaritans have despised each other for years —it's a long story. For many reasons, they think we Samaritans are unclean, not real Jews. One big problem is that we worship differently, in different places. We worship here at Mt. Gerazim, but their temple is in Jerusalem.

As I trudge on toward the well, I encounter a group of several men, heading in the opposite direction. They are strangers who look like Jews, and I wonder idly what they are doing in Samaritan territory. As I pass them, they avert their eyes and do not speak, but I hear them talking about the provisions they're planning to buy in town.

I round the last bend in the road to the well and see someone sitting beside it. Who in the world can it be, out here in the middle of the day? As I come closer I can tell that the person is a man dressed in a homespun robe dusty from travel.

When I arrive at the well, the man stands up with a smile. The minute I see his face with its deep set dark eyes and strong nose I can tell that he is Jewish. "Please," he says, "give me a drink." The well is at least 100 ft. deep, far too deep for him to get it himself, and apparently he is as alone as I am.

"Sir, how is it that you ask me, a Samaritan woman, to give you a drink? You know that Jews and Samaritans have nothing to do with each other." I am aware that Jews have all kinds of rules and he is breaking at least two of them. They believe that anything we Samaritans touch is automatically unclean. This means he shouldn't touch, let alone drink, from a cup I've handled. And besides, Jewish men don't speak with women in public at all.

Then he speaks again. "If you knew the gift of God, and who is asking you for a drink, you would ask me for living water."

What kind of answer is this? Living water is fresh, running water, and the water in the well is still, but I just say, "You have no bucket and the well is deep. How will you get living water?"

Again, his answer goes right past my question. "Everyone who drinks of this water will get thirsty again, but those who drink of the water I will give them will never be thirsty. The water I give will become in them a spring of water gushing up to eternal life."

The conversation is growing stranger and stranger, but I feel a sense of awe and wonder surging in my heart. Who is this man, and what kind of water is he speaking of? He must mean something far greater than the ordinary water we drink, even greater than that which comes from a flowing stream. Imagine having my real thirst quenched, the thirst I feel for life and hope. I can't help exclaiming, "Sir, give me this water, so that I may never be thirsty or have to keep coming here to draw water."

But suddenly the man changes direction. Instead of going on about water, he says, "Call your husband, and come back."

I don't know why he's changing the subject, but decide to be straight with him. "I have no husband."

"Yes, you are right. You have had five husbands and the man you have now is not your husband."

My heart lurches, and I catch my breath. How can he know about my life and speak with such certainty? It's as if he's looking right inside me, and it feels pretty uncomfortable. When I recover myself enough to speak, I decide to change the subject away from my personal life and go back to talking about religion. Worship differences between Jews and Samaritans ought to be safe. I say, "Sir, I see that you are a prophet. Our ancestors worshipped here on this mountain, But you say that people must worship in Jerusalem."

He answers in his authoritative way, "Woman, the hour is coming when you will worship not on this mountain, or in Jerusalem. The hour is coming and now is when true worshippers will worship in spirit and truth. God is spirit and those who worship God must worship in spirit and truth."

Now I realize that this man is absolutely unique—a prophet, yes, yet far more than a prophet. He knows what he's talking about and is telling the truth. Marvelous! Just think, he is saying that the old barriers are coming down. Samaritans and Jews and all people will be able to worship the one true God together! I respond with the little bit of teaching I've heard. "I know that Messiah is coming, the one who is called the Christ. When he comes he will proclaim all things to us."

Looking deeply into my eyes, the man says, "I am he, the man who is speaking to you."

He has revealed me to myself and now he is revealing himself to me. He is the Messiah! I lean back against the well, overcome with amazement.

The man and I are so focused on our conversation that we do not hear anyone coming, but just then, some men come striding up to the well. It's the same group I saw earlier. They look at the man, obviously their leader, and then at me, with astonishment and distaste. They don't ask any questions, but their expressions say it all. "Why in the world is our teacher polluting himself by talking to a woman, and a Samaritan at that?"

I don't want to stay around until they leave, so I turn to go. Abandoning my empty water bucket beside the well, I hurry back to the village, now scarcely feeling the heat in my excitement. Something about the way the man talked with me, took me seriously and understood me, frees me from worrying about how people might react to my story. My need to tell them about this amazing man who knows everything about me and taught me so much crowds out every other consideration. I don't care what anyone thinks. To everyone I see I exclaim, "Come, see a man who told me everything I have ever done! He can't be the Messiah, can he?" I watch as people look up at me in surprise and then start heading toward Jacob's well.

Later I hear that the man's name is Jesus, and that many people start believing in him because of my testimony. Then some Samaritans ask him to stay with them, and he stops in the village for two days. Many more see and hear for themselves, and come to believe that Jesus is the Messiah, Savior of the world.

As for me, the more I reflect on what Jesus said to me that day at the well, the more deeply I believe in him and his teaching. From that one encounter and conversation I feel that I know him well enough to trust him with my life. And more, his kindness, insight and acceptance have helped me to change my life and find more acceptance among the people of my village.

Now I can say and believe the last verse of my favorite psalm, "Why are you cast down, O my soul and why are you disquieted within me? Hope in God; for I shall again praise you, my help and my God."

And more, now I experience the presence of Jesus' Spirit daily. It is indeed living water, flowing through my life and assuaging my thirst. May you also come to know him and drink so deeply that you never thirst again.

9

LOST AND FOUND

(Based on Luke 15:11-24)

What a drag it is to live in this household! Up at the crack of dawn, work all day, early to bed, prayers on schedule, meals on the dot. It's the kind of home they call "well-ordered," but it is enough to drive you crazy.

No variety, no action, no fun! Life is passing me by fast. Here I am, seventeen. I want to get out, see the world. I certainly don't want to hang around home, with my older brother, James, lording it over me all the time. Mr. Perfect, that's him! He is sickeningly good, without a rebellious bone in his body. I don't think he's ever talked back, and I doubt he even wants to. He always does everything right, a "chip off the old block," as they say. But to me he's just boring, just like life at home. Bor-ing.

And my father? I try to respect him, to honor him as the commandment says, but I can't understand why he likes to live like this. He has the money. Why doesn't he ever spend it on a little excitement? I know I'm a puzzle to him—he actually likes our life. He can't understand how trapped I feel. He tries to be patient when I rant and rave, but he's always so reasonable, so rational, it makes me even madder. I wish that just once he'd shout at me, let me know he really cares about something.

But instead he just reasons with me patiently. "Joshua, you are so lucky to have a fine home and family that loves you. You even have an inheritance coming your way. I wish you could be happy to settle down and work with me and James."

When he talks like that I just want to yell. "Don't you see I'm different. I want different things. I don't care what you say, this is my life. My life! Leave me alone and go ahead with yours."

I've never dared to go that far, but I know he feels sad when I complain. What can I do to get out of this cage and start living? Every day I rack my brains, and finally I come up with a plan. I will ask him for my inheritance, now.

Carefully, I plan my strategy. I am not asking anything against the law or custom, but I need to think about how to present the idea to my father. It is not unheard of in our world for a son to receive his inheritance early. But it is unusual to ask for a final settlement, one which would allow me to dispose of property as well as using it. But how else would I be able to lead an independent life, free of all strings?

One night after a good dinner I finally get up the courage to speak to my father. I knock on his door, and ask if I can talk with him about something serious. "Come in, my son, sit down."

I sit on the edge of my chair and lean forward as I speak. "Father, you know I'm not like James. I don't want to spend my life farming this land. I beg you to give me my inheritance now, so I can go out into the world and make my own fortune, my own life."

For a long moment, my father sits silent, looking me in the eye. "This is hard for me, Joshua, you are so young, only seventeen. It has always been my dream for you and James to work this land together after I am gone. Have you thought and prayed about it? Are you sure?"

It is hard for me to keep my cool. Here I am, suffocating, gasping for a gulp of air in this house, and he asks if I'm sure. I manage to stay polite. "I know your dream, father, but I have dreams too. I need to go out on my own, I must go. I am sure, completely sure."

I see my father's face fall, and then resolve into lines of resignation. "My dear son, I can see that you are determined. You may have your inheritance."

To my everlasting amazement he is actually saying "Yes." I can hardly believe it! I go over and give him a hug, crying "Thank you—you won't be sorry."

I don't want to give father time to change his mind, so the very next morning I pack a few things. I don't need much, I certainly don't plan to wear these country clothes when I get to the city.

I go to my father, and true to his word, he gives me the money. Of course my share does not include any of the land I'm not going to work. He walks to the door with me, looking sorrowful. James comes to say goodbye too, but he looks more angry than sad. "I hope you know what you're doing, and what this is doing to our father."

"Father's all right with it. He understands." James just shakes his head and goes inside.

I turn and start down the road. I'm actually leaving. Heading for Tyre, a real city. I feel so happy, so free, as if I've sprouted wings.

The first thing I do when I hit the city is to buy some clothes to fit my new life. Then I set out to meet some people to hang out with. It is so easy—I find new drinking buddies everywhere I go, and women flock around me, jostling for my time and attention. I spend my money freely on everybody. We party all night and sleep all day. At last I am living! No more of that "early to bed, early to rise" nonsense.

After two years of fantastically riotous living I notice that the old bank balance is getting low. "Oh well," I think, "something is bound to turn up. How can I miss with my great friends, this big city? Who knows what wonderful things are in store for me?"

Then, going into the third year, drought hits the area hard, followed by famine. Everything goes into recession. The partying is over. My funds are almost gone, and nothing, no loans, no gifts, no nothing comes my way. I have to get work. Most of my friends have disappeared, and those who are left don't give me any leads. Some won't even pass the time of day anymore. I begin to get desperate. I sell my few valuables and most of my clothes.

Finally, I look around in the countryside and find a job with a farmer as a swine herd. It couldn't be worse. Can you imagine a nice Jewish boy working in a pig pen? With all those unclean animals? I've never been big on my father's religion, but this is too much. I keep remembering the teaching, "Cursed is the man who keeps swine."

Cursed. That's me all right. Barefoot in the mud, clothing in rags, doing filthy work. And I am so hungry! I could eat some of the carob beans we give the pigs, but I just can't. They are too disgusting. No one in the farmer's household gives me much of anything to eat either, so I am in a bad way.

What have I come to, the son of a fine family? I've squandered my inheritance and have absolutely nothing. I am starving, wallowing with the pigs like an unclean animal myself. And on top of everything I am desperately lonely, deserted by my so-called friends. I have no one, no one at all.

It is when I hit bottom, when I see and feel nothing but bad news about myself and my situation, that I seem to wake up. I see a new possibility. I say to myself, "I do have someone, I will leave this cursed place and go to my father. I will go home." Suddenly, that place which had seemed to dull, so stifling, looks full of hope, comfort and promise. Home!

Of course I have no claim on my father any more. I know that. And I can imagine what my brother, Mr. Perfect, will say when he sees me, but I determine to go. My only option is to throw myself on my father's mercy. I will tell him how wrong I've been. Maybe he'll let me work for room and board along with the rest of his servants. Maybe. O please, maybe!

All the long way home I rehearse my speech. "Father, I have sinned against heaven and against you. I no longer deserve to be called your son, treat me as one of your paid servants." I practice the words over and over as I trudge along, hoping against hope that he will not turn me away.

By the time the house comes into view, my stomach is curled up in a knot. What possessed me to come home? How can I dare to knock on that door? Then I see a figure a long way off. He is standing near the entrance to the house, where the olive grove begins. He seems to be looking toward the road—peering into the distance—straining to see who is approaching in barefeet and rags. It is my father.

Then all of a sudden he starts running, long robes flapping around him. What a sight—that dignified patriarch huffing and puffing with all the exertion. What a sight indeed! My father is running to meet me. He hurtles to me and gathers me up in a fierce embrace. "O Joshua, it is you. My son, my dear son!"

I extricate myself from his arms and throw myself down at his feet. I try to start my speech, "Father, I'm no longer worthy…" but he pulls me up by both hands, bellowing orders to the servants. "Hurry, bring him the best robe. Put a signet ring on his finger. Get some sandals for his feet, for heaven's sake. He is a son of this house, not some slave to be going go barefoot! And kill that calf we've been saving for the high holidays. This is better than any holiday. We will eat and make merry, for this, my son, was lost, and is found!"

His love is amazing! Unbelievable! My father is receiving me, forgiving me, embracing me. He is accepting me just as I am—messy inside and out. It is nothing less than a miracle.

Am I sorry I went off the way I did? It's hard to say. It was so painful for everyone. But if I hadn't, I might never have know what is really important in life. I might never have realized what I really want, and how much I am loved. If I had not been lost, could I have been found?

10

HOMECOMING

(Based on Luke 15:11-32)

INTRODUCTION

In the 15th chapter of Luke's Gospel, Jesus tells three parables of the lost which teach of God's seeking and forgiving love. They are "The Lost Sheep," "The Lost Coin," and "The Prodigal or Lost Son".

Today's sermon is on the third and most complex parable which deals deeply with forgiveness. In recognition of the father's role, it is sometimes called "The Forgiving Father." Recently, some scholars have stressed the fact that the story has not two, but three, important characters, by speaking of it as the parable of "The Father Who Had Two Sons." Today, we'll be thinking of all three members of the family.

As always, I include some historical background and some additions that seem true to the story. Here, one of these is the thought that the mother of the two sons died when they were very young. People often ask me where she is. Scripture does not mention her at all, perhaps reflecting the patriarchal structure of the family at that time, but speaking of her death gives another possible explanation for her absence from the narrative.

This morning's first person story sermon is given from the point of view of the father, but I hope that as you hear him speak, you will think about the two sons as well. Ask yourself which character you identify with most. And please consider what it means to be forgiven, to forgive, and to refuse to forgive in your life.

HOMECOMING

Every day I try to be a good father. I am blessed with two sons and try hard to do right by them both. Their mother died when they were very young and it hasn't been easy bringing them up. Even now, when they are young men, it's hard to be even-handed, to let them know how much I love them both.

They couldn't be more different. James seems to have been born old—old and responsible. He is ultra serious and seems to look down on fun as beneath his dignity. I used to worry about him having a real childhood. Instead of playing, he used to come down into the fields, tagging after me. He would bend down and pick up the biggest hoe—twice as tall as he was—and struggle to use it. Later he liked to come into my office and stand by my desk as I worked on accounts. "What are you doing, Father? What are you writing? How do you keep track of all those papers?" Even his games were serious—pretending he was in charge, giving orders to servants, making lists of supplies he'd need for some project.

James always seemed to understand and bear the burden of being the elder brother. Now that he's older, it is a joy to have such a devoted, interested, hardworking son. I feel his deep rooted love and concern for me and the fruitful land which will one day be his responsibility. At the same time, I have to admit that James is easy to forget about—to ignore and take for granted. Nothing he does demands my attention. He never gives me a moment's worry, trouble or grief. Never, that is, until now.

My younger son, Joshua, is another story. From day one he's been a handful, a fussy baby and mischievous child. He always seems to be in trouble. What <u>he</u> wants is his top value. "I'll do what I want when I want to," he'd chant as he tore around the property.

He doesn't seem to care much for the things our family values –faith, hard work, respect, loyalty, obedience. As he grew older, I was probably far too soft with him. James seemed to grow in the right direction without much guidance, and I just assumed Joshua would do the same. I should have clamped down harder, drawn the line more clearly, been tougher. But I didn't, and have to accept that now. By nature I'm not a harsh disciplinarian. I just expect people to do the right thing.

On top of this, how can anyone clamp down on Joshua? He disarms everyone—a real charmer with his wide smile, spontaneity and sense of fun. He knows how to get what he wants too, how to use honey instead of vinegar to get his way. No tantrums for Joshua. He cajoles, and persuades and flatters. Often I try to be stern, even angry, when he gets out of line, only to end up laughing. How he delights me! And manipulates me. Any discipline I do exert rolls right off his back. He can woo himself back into my good graces with a smile, a hug, and a rueful "I'm sorry." He'd be perfect in politics.

Now entering his late teens, Joshua is growing even more rebellious, and I am more and more concerned. What will he do with himself, what can he make of his life? He hates working our land. "Boring," is his verdict. He has trouble buckling down to anything except partying with local ne'er do wells, and making fun of his brother's serious ways. "Sober sides," "Mr. Perfect," he calls him. "James is missing out," he decrees, "wasting the best years of his life. I'm going make the most of my youth, live while I can really enjoy it."

I can't help wondering, "What does he have in mind?" and it isn't long before I find out.

One evening, after dinner, Joshua knocks on my office door and I invite him in. He is wearing his most engaging smile and a respectful attitude. "May I come in, Father? I have something important to ask you."

"What does he want this time?" I think as I invite him to come in, and begin to feel that smile melting my defenses.

"Father, please, I want you to give me my share of our property, my inheritance—one third of everything." I think fleetingly, this boy has done his homework. He knows that our Jewish law gives two-thirds to the eldest son. And his request isn't really outrageous. After all, a lot of fathers give early title to their sons instead of requiring them to wait to inherit. Like many younger sons, Joshua may want to use his share to emigrate and lead an independent life. I don't like the idea much—he lacks the maturity and direction to handle an inheritance. He's not even out of his teens and is no good at applying himself at anything worthwhile—can he possibly handle life on his own? Besides, even though I wouldn't mind letting go of the property, how can I let go of him, the joy of my life? What will I do without him—the laughter and noise, music and mischief? My heart lurches at the thought.

Later, I wish I had followed common sense and said "no." or at least, "wait." But how, after a lifetime of "yeses" can I suddenly say "no." How can I, who has never denied him anything, deny this great wish? So I go ahead, say "yes" and divide my property between my sons. Then it's goodbye to Joshua.

His "I'm outa here" attitude distresses me. He can't seem to leave fast enough. The first thing he does it to convert his portion of the property to cash. How it hurts to see him do that! Usually when a son gets early title, he only invests and uses the property. He doesn't dispose of it. That way, his father's livelihood is assured during his lifetime, and the capital is preserved for the next generation. Converting it to cash is like saying I'm already dead—that he has no more responsibility for me. He is breaking his ties, saying "no" to his birthright, his history, even his God. He is rejecting everything he has been and is. He is choosing to be dead to me.

Cash in hand, Joshua leaves, without even saying goodbye to James. "Sorry. I can't wait till he comes in from the fields. I have to get going." He picks up the bag he has filled with a few favorite belongings, gives me a brief hug and is out the door. I watch his jaunty, determined figure striding down the road toward the city. He grows smaller, until my eyes strain for a glimpse. Finally, I see him no more. He is gone, leaving nothing but a great hole in my heart.

At first I hope that Joshua will write, or send some sort of message, just a word to say he's all right. But nothing. One or two travelers tell me they've heard he is having a great time, a riotous time, in the city. These reports do nothing to reassure me, but make me feel uneasier than ever. If they are right, it sounds as if he is just wasting his money instead of using it to get started in life. I know I am still too involved with him and should let it go. I try to detach, to concentrate on this place, and especially James. But I am consumed by the loss of Joshua. Not a day goes by that I do not think of him, picture his face in my mind, yearn for him, commend him to God's care. If you have ever had a dear child become estranged, go off, disappear, you know what I'm talking about. Nothing alleviates the pain. For me, functioning normally means submerging the constant ache, the fearful imaginings, the long sorrow. How I hope and pray that Joshua has pulled himself together and begun to build a life, that he has not become one more victim of big city life.

One year, two years, of silence, and increasing fear as terrible famine spreads and holds much of our world in its grip. Then, this morning, I am out tending our olive trees. I love their soft, feathery, gray-green foliage. It looks as if we will have a fine crop this year. As I work, I glance up and notice someone walking along the road, a long way off.

We're not expecting any visitors. Idly, I wonder who it is—probably someone on going on to the neighboring farm. I go back to my inspecting the olive trees. When I look up again, the figure has come closer and definitely turned toward our place. I freeze, my eyes struggling to bridge the distance. Whoever it is moves slowly, hesitantly, yet something about his walk seems familiar. Can it be? How can it be…Joshua? Soon there is no doubt.

My heart reaches out, leaps out, toward him. All the anger and hurt and worry I have lived with for so long dissolves into joy and expectation. Compassion and forgiveness flood my whole being. He is coming home, actually coming home. All I want to do is to welcome him.

I know it's not done. I know it's undignified for a man of my age and status to run, but I can't wait. I take off as fast as I can, stiff knees protesting, sleeves billowing, robe flapping.

When I reach him, Joshua falls down on his knees before me, and starts to speak in a tone I've never heard before. "Father, I have sinned against heaven and before you. I am no longer worthy to be called your son."

I take both of his hands and pull him to his feet, enfolding him in my arms. "Hush now, hush, my dear, dear son." I step back a bit so I can see him. What a sight he is—dirty, skinny, barefoot, wearing rags. And oh, the smell!

I shout for the servants and they come running. I issue orders, "Quickly. Bring Joshua a fine robe and a signet ring for his finger; after all, he is a son of this house. Bring sandals befitting his status as a free man, and go, kill the fatted calf we have been saving for the high holidays. Let us eat and drink and make merry, for this, my son, was dead and is alive again. He was lost and is found!"

I want the whole household to join in the celebration, and before long we are gathered. It is a wonderful party, filled with joy and laughter. His face filled with amazement, Joshua stands at the center. He has cleaned up well, and though pale and thin, seems to be regaining some of his smiling spirit.

The banquet is over, and the dogs have retired to quiet corners with their prize bones and other tasty morsels. I am leaning back in my chair, content to relax and watch the dancing, when a trusted servant comes over and whispers in my ear, "Master, I'm sorry to bother you, but it's Mr. James. A few minutes ago he came in from a long day in the fields and asked what is going on. I told him that Mr. Joshua is back and that we're having a celebration, but he won't come in. He's outside, and very angry."

Oh no, in my joy and excitement I had actually forgotten my other son. Maybe he is right. Maybe I just don't give him the same kind of thought I give to Joshua, the same level of concern. I did not even send someone out to fetch him for the banquet. He had to hear about Joshua's return from one of the servants when he came in at the usual time. How could I do such a thing? How could I be so thoughtless? I spring to my feet and rush outside, hoping to calm James, to bring him in to join the party.

I have seen James angry, but never this angry. His hurt and rage erupt in words that pelt me like sharp stones. "All these years, all these years. I work for you like a slave every day. I always respect you, never disobey you, never question your authority. And yet you have never given me so much as a young goat—let alone a fatted calf—so I can celebrate with my friends. But now, when this son of yours comes back, this son who has devoured your property with prostitutes, now for him you kill the fatted calf."

This is old anger, deep anger. Clearly it has been festering in his heart a long, long time. All these years James has been laboring to earn my love, unaware that it is his already. When Joshua left he must have sensed my emptiness and despair. He must have felt frustrated and inadequate because he couldn't seem to fill the hole in my heart. My mourning made him believe that I love Joshua best. James must be yearning for some sign, some spontaneous gesture that expresses my love for him, my approval and appreciation for his responsible work and faithful care. It's true, doing such a thing never occurred to me—he is just with me day by day, steady and dependable. I can always count on him. How could I be so blind, so insensitive? No one wants to be taken for granted.

I reach out and gently touch James' arm, but he brushes my hand away. "Oh James," I moan, "my dear son, forgive me. You are always with me, and all that I have is yours. We have to celebrate and make merry, for this brother of yours was dead, and is alive; he was lost and is found."

I stand there in the darkness, pleading with James, appealing to his sense of natural connection, inviting him to come in and join the celebration. I know that I am acting undignified again, that fathers do not plead with their sons anymore than they run to meet them, but isn't relationship more important than rules? I am unwilling to regain one son, only to lose the other. James is so good, so faithful. If only he can realize, and believe that there's plenty of room in my heart for both of my boys. If only he can unbend, forgive, feel the same joy I do in his brother's return. If only he will let go of his righteousness long enough to come in to the party and dance.

I may forgive too quickly, without asking enough. But I'd rather do that, than wrap myself in a shroud of hurt and anger. Shrouds are for the dead. If James continues to do that, pitying himself and judging his brother, we can never be a family again. Can't he see that being family is more important than who's right and who's wrong? How I hope he will let the healing lubrication of forgiveness flow into his heart. Surely it is good to forgive and forget and start over.

I say my piece as we stand there in the shadow of the house, hearing the sound of music and revelry inside. When I finish, James just stares at me for a moment. Then he shakes his head, turns away without a word and starts walking slowly toward the olive grove. I stay outside awhile, but he does not come back. There is nothing to do but to go back inside and wait, as I am doing now.

Perhaps James would like me to choose between him and Joshua, but I'm not going to do that. As I told you, despite my mistakes, I've spent my life trying to be a good father to both sons. Rejecting one would deny the meaning of my life. No. The choice is up to him.

I don't know what James will do. He is a hard man—a man of principle. He doesn't even realize that with his unforgiving spirit he is just as lost as Joshua ever was. I have no idea if he will be able to let go of his anger and accept my invitation. Is it possible for him to take the risk of forgiving and come in to share the joy of finding and being found? I just don't know.

If you were James, what would you do?

11

ON NOT LOSING HEART

(Luke 18:1-8, II Corinthians 4:16--5:7)

I tried everything else I could think of before I went to see that judge. I know that he has the reputation of being tough. Besides, the judges Herod or the Romans choose for us are usually corrupt—we even call them robber judges. They certainly don't buy into our Jewish tradition of concern for the needy. You have to have the money for a bribe or the right friends to get very far with these men, and I have neither, but I was determined to try anyway. You see my step-son, Caleb, is trying to claim not only my husband's whole estate, but also the remaining portion of my dowry, the part which is supposed to return to me when my husband dies.

During his last illness, my husband said, "I love you, Sarah, and don't want you to suffer the way so many widows do. I plan to have you inherit part of my estate as well as your dowry, and will tell Caleb how much to settle on you."

Well, I'm sure he did tell him, but now Caleb says "He never said any such thing!" And he tells me that he plans to take my marriage portion as well. "For unexpected expenses," he says, without delineating them. It's just my word against his, and if Caleb succeeds, I will have nothing to live on, nothing at all, and I don't look forward to starving. I am only 34 years old and hope to have many more years of living ahead of me.

In our world life isn't easy for widows. As a class we stand at the bottom of the social totem pole, and are a symbol of powerlessness and vulnerability. We are the classic victims, ripe for exploitation at every turn. Oh yes, our tradition of caring for the needy requires people to offer us and orphans minimum assistance, but in return, widows are expected to keep their place, always quiet, submissive and grateful. Accepting charity feels demeaning to me, since I know I have resources that are legally mine. I have no intention of living as a charity case and refuse to back off, to keep silent.

But so far the powers are siding with my step-son who has the double advantage of being born male and a promising young member of the community. But Caleb doesn't have my motivation. I am determined to get justice, to claim what is legally mine.

The sun is shining and the air feels soft with spring as I enter the courthouse to see the judge for the first time. Maybe, like the earth, I can make a new beginning. I stand at the great door of the judge's chamber, gathering my courage. Finally, I raise my fist and knock firmly.

"Come in," growls a harsh voice.

Swallowing my fear, I push open the heavy door and go in. The judge looks up from the desk where he is writing something. His eyes narrow and his mouth turns down in a scowl as he sees me, a mere woman and a widow to boot.

"Yes," he barks, "Who are you and what do you want?"

I know he expects me to cower before him, but I stand up straight with my shoulders back and speak in a strong voice. "Your Honor, I am Sarah, the widow of Adam ben Abram, who died last month. My step-son, Caleb, is claiming my husband's whole estate and the remainder of my dowry as well. My husband wanted me to have a portion of his estate, and the dowry is legally mine. I have nothing else to live on."

"Hmph," said the judge. "Well, your step-son is probably right. You can only make such a claim if your husband willed it that way and wrote it down."

"But Your Honor, my husband died unexpectedly and hadn't finished writing his will. Still, even if you deny me any of his estate, our law says that a woman owns her dowry and can reclaim it when her husband dies. All I want is justice."

I see redness creeping up the judge's neck as his face flushes with anger. "Ha! You presume to tell me about the law! You dare to speak to me of justice! Begone, woman, and stop your sniveling."

I turn and leave. There is no point in trying to say more when the judge is so angry.

A few days pass before I stand before that imposing door and knock a second time. I present myself before the judge again, saying, "Your honor, all I want is justice. Please hear my plea."

What does he do but turn his back on me without a word!

I leave again, but I refuse to lose heart and give up. I keep on going day after day. I'm never rude—always respectful, but persistent. I know my cause is just and keep saying over and over, "All I want is justice."

After two weeks of this, I wonder if the judge will have me thrown out of his chamber bodily, or even arrested. Sometimes he turns his back, but sometimes he glances at me. He always refuses to speak to me, but occasionally shakes his head "no,." Gradually I notice a change in his behavior. Instead of reddening with anger every time he sees me coming, the judge just sits quietly, with a resigned look on his face. Maybe he's realizing that he'll never get rid of me unless he does something.

Finally, after another week of my visits, the judge exclaims, "OK, OK. I'll grant your request. Not because you're right. Not because it's just. No. I'll say yes to you because I want to get rid of you.

You'll keep working me over, pummeling me, forever. Next thing I know you'll give me a black eye!"

He bends over his writing desk and quickly scribbles an order giving me my marriage portion and a small percentage of my husband's estate as well.

As he hands me the precious document, I cry, "Thank you, Judge. Thank you so much. Now I can keep on living. And I am.

* * * * *

Luke says that Jesus told this story to teach us not to lose heart and to keep on praying. It was meant to encourage Christians who were living in the shadow of persecution and tired of waiting and wondering when the Lord would return to set everything right. This situation is what Paul is thinking of in our passage from II Corinthians too.

Scholars call the story of the widow and the judge a parable of contrast. If persistence can persuade even such a cruel and corrupt judge to do justice, how much more will our good God care for us when we pray diligently in a spirit of faith and trust.

What does the story say about our prayer life? What does it assume about God and prayer? What kind of attitude of mind and heart and spirit does prayer require?

First, it says something about God. Our God is not some abstract force or power, but eternal, personal Spirit. Although we experience the Spirit within ourselves, God is not limited to dwelling within us. God has a personal reality beyond ourselves, and is a real as our dearest family member or friend.

All through the Biblical story, God reaches out for relationship—taking the initiative, speaking to people and expecting their response. When God actually comes among us in Jesus, we see how much God longs to live in relationship with us. And Jesus makes it clear that we can communicate directly with God in prayer.

God opens the door wide and invites us to come near. When we pray we aren't approaching some cranky and unjust judge. We don't have to have the right connections or a bribe in hand. We don't even have to say the right words. Jesus promises that God will hear us, because God, the trustworthy One, loves us and wants to hear and respond.

So first, prayer assumes that God is real and personal, the dear One who invites us to engage in conversation. Second, prayer assumes that we need to pray. When we come to God out of the full reality of our lives, out of our struggles and hopes and yearnings, we are needy.

Intense need is what one black pastor felt when he said, "Unless you've stood for years, knocking at a locked door, your knuckles bleeding, you do not really know what prayer is." Have you ever felt that way when you've prayed? Have your prayers been a persistent and painful asking, seeking and knocking?

Surely it was that way for the widow. She was totally vulnerable, at the end of her rope, when she went to that cruel judge. We may not be as desperate as she, but it is essential to recognize our need when we come before God. This is what Jesus meant when he said, "Blessed are the poor in spirit." He was speaking of those who know their need for God. If you feel you've "got it made" and can handle everything yourself, you are blind to your need and cannot pray from the heart.

Prayer assumes the reality of a personal God who wants to communicate with us and springs from a healthy sense of need. Third, it requires an attitude of expectation—what the parable calls "faith on earth." The widow expected that judge to do justice. Because of this she persisted, and like her, we are supposed to expect something to happen when we pray.

At the same time, one of our problems in prayer comes from expecting the wrong thing. We think that God will do our will. Then, if what we want is not forthcoming, we doubt that God answers prayer. We get discouraged, even cynical. I remember sitting next to a man on a plane who took me on the minute he realized I was a minister. "How can you people believe in prayer, anyway? You give God so many excuses. First you say God answers prayer, but when you don't get what you want, you say that your request isn't God's will. You always get God off the hook."

From a secular point of view, the man was right. It takes deep faith and Christian maturity to see that God does hear and does answer even when the answer is "no," or something different from our request.

From childhood on, my college roommate and dear friend, Edie, knew she would probably get cancer. It had afflicted the female line of her family for generations. She was scrupulous about having regular medical exams and kept up on new treatments as they became available.

Despite her care, when she was in her 40's cancer cells began to grow. She had a double mastectomy. When she had chemo she was very hopeful, but after a time in remission the cancer came back. This time it attacked her ovaries, stomach and liver, and kept spreading throughout her body. For over five years, she tried all kinds of treatments but the disease was unstoppable.

As her health deteriorated, so did Edie's faith. Why had this happened when she'd been so careful? She'd always been a devoted Christian—how could God ignore her prayers and fail to cure her? Didn't God care about her and her family? How would they cope without her--her youngest was not yet in junior high. She prayed and prayed, even bargaining with God. "If only you let me live till Chris graduates from High School I'll be the best Christian you ever saw."

The cancer kept spreading and Edie grew furious with God—this God who might or might not exist, but who definitely did not care. We who loved her kept on praying, but she lost heart and stopped. Still, God didn't give up on Edie. Gradually, as she lay in bed, hairless and hurting, she began to feel the touch of the Holy Spirit moving in her heart. Peace began to fill her as she accepted what could not be changed and realized that God was loving and helping her right there in the midst of her pain. She was able to release her fear and place her family in God's care.

We could see the change. Instead of anger and bitterness, now we sensed a profound serenity in Edie. Everyone who visited her left comforted, lifted, even energized. The last days of her life and her brave death became a living picture of faith and love.

Most of my life I have trusted that God answers prayer, even though the answers weren't always what I hoped for. But during that painful time, I began to understand that being healed is not the same as being cured. Edie's cancer was not cured, but surely God healed her, and through her, helped and healed many.

We believe in a personal, eternal God who listens and answers prayer. When we pray out of our deepest needs and persist patiently, we can expect God to respond to us, with hope and healing. And so it is, we walk by faith, not sight, and we do not lose heart. We do not lose heart.

12

COME DOWN!

(Based on Luke 19:1-10)

Today I want to tell you about a meeting that changed my life.

My name is Zaccheaus, I live in Palestine and am the chief tax collector for Jericho. I'm a Jew, but I work for the Romans. Yes, you heard right—the Romans.

Actually, we Jews live in a world dominated by Romans. They levy taxes on just about everything. It's 1% on income, 10% on grain. There's even a tax for just existing. Then there are duties to pay on the use of the roads. If you drive a cart, you pay on each wheel. Your friendly neighborhood tax collector has a lucrative job. The Romans sell the right to collect taxes to the highest bidder. The chosen collector has to send in a basic assessment, but anything beyond that is gravy and there are no rules about what he can charge. We have little communication between towns, so people don't know what others are paying.

What a game! We learn all the tricks and lend money at high interest as a sideline. It's no surprise that we tax collectors become rich—rich and hated. We are seen as traitors too, because we serve the Romans.

For a long time I loved raking in all that money and wielding power in the community, but about a year ago the excitement began to pall. I have no close family or friends and am an outcast in the Jewish community. The leaders decree that tax collectors are unclean, so I'm not welcome in the synagogue. It wouldn't do for me to touch someone. They lump me with murderers and robbers—well, I guess I am a robber of sorts. It isn't too bad to be ignored, but to be actively disliked feels miserable.

I begin wondering what life is about anyway. I have everything I need, and more, but it doesn't seem to add up. I want something else, but I don't know what. When I go into homes to collect taxes, sometimes I feel so lonely that I linger and try to talk. Of course I'm not welcome, but people fear me, and don't dare tell me to leave.

One evening a steward told me about a traveling rabbi named Jesus. He is going to pass through Jericho on his way to Jerusalem. Apparently he is causing quite a stir because he insists on mixing with the common folk—even riff-raff—and sits down to eat with prostitutes and other sinners. He spends a lot of time teaching and healing, even on the Sabbath. Strange behavior for a rabbi! What interests me the most is that this rabbi is said to have a tax collector named Matthew among his followers. Astounding! Rabbis teach that tax collectors are sinners, and no rabbi has given me the time of day for years. If this rabbi, this Jesus, is different, maybe—just maybe—he'll talk to me. Maybe he will listen to my story and help me find something to care about, to live for.... MAYBE!

Well, it seems that Jesus is due in Jericho the very next day. I sit up late, thinking, making plans. There will be a lot of people waiting to greet him. How can I manage to meet him? I hate crowds. It is just too easy for people to vent their anger in a crowd—pushing, pinching, even stepping on me—and then pretending it is a mistake. Besides, I'm very short, so I never can see, and no one will let me through. What to do?

Finally I decide to leave home very early and beat the crowd. I get up and out at dawn, but as I near the Jericho gate I see that I am already too late. Many people are already gathered and milling around. There is no way I can see Jesus in that mob—much less talk with him.

But I have to—I have to find a way. Somehow my interest in the man has grown into an urgent desire. I simply must see him. Maybe I can put my sleeved arm over my face and make it to the front of the crowd without being recognized. Then I see a better solution, right next to me. It is a small sycamore tree overlooking the road. Before anyone notices me, I scramble up and settle into a crook between two branches. The leaves shield me from view, but I can see everything.

Before long I see Jesus and his followers coming toward the city gate. They are walking slowly, paying attention to the people as they pass by. Jesus looks around and smiles. As they come nearer, I see that he is more than superficially friendly. He looks at everyone sharply, carefully. His eyes seem to see into people, to know what is going on inside each person.

They are very close to my tree now. I wonder if I have the courage to jump down and speak to him. It would be hard, in front of all these people. If only I could find out where he is staying and visit him there—speak to him alone. If only God would help me find a way. But I have forgotten how to pray.

As all these wonderings swirl through my head, I hear a voice calling—a voice calling my name. "Come down, Zacchaeus. Zacchaeus, come down." Lo and behold, Jesus is calling me! It is hard to believe he means me, but there is no question about it. He is peering up through the leaves, looking straight at me. And his look and tone, are not a request, but a command.

"Come down, Zacchaeus. I'm staying at your house today."

I feel a tremendous tension. I want to speak to this rabbi, but now I am terrified. What does he want from me? But I climb down and stand before him.

"Yes, rabbi, you are calling me?"

His eyes catch and hold me. It is as if he is seeing inside me. As if he knows everything I have ever been, said, done. I feel naked, exposed, before those intense dark eyes. I cannot hide. The evil of my life is laid bare before the goodness of this One who is calling me. And yet, what had he said? "Come down, because I'm staying at your house today."

How can this be? My heart turns over. How can this amazing man see into me? Through me? And still want to come to my house? Wonder and gratitude flood my heart. He knows who I am, what I am, and yet he wants to be with me, to visit my home, to share with me.

What a gift! What an undeserved, joyous gift!

I think I am in some sort of shock. Something within me is turning around—turning away from the dishonesty, the game playing, the cheating. I feel a deep longing to participate in the kind of goodness present in this commanding, accepting individual. I am turning my back on the old Zacchaeus, and beginning to feel a new Zacchaeus emerging into being.

Finally I speak. "Thank you, Rabbi. Thank you from the bottom of my heart. You do me great honor, and you are welcome, more than welcome, to come to my home today."

Only then do I become aware of the crowd muttering angrily. "Some teacher this is—inviting himself to the house of the worst sinner in town! Why doesn't he want to come to my house?" "Or mine, or mine," the rumbling continued. "Why doesn't he visit anyone other than that crook, Zacchaeus?"

But Jesus doesn't seem to care. As I watch him react, I realize that what I'd heard about him is true. This Jesus isn't like the other rabbis and religious leaders. He cares about everyone, even those no one else will speak to.

I feel a sense of newness, of power, swelling within me. I want to let Jesus know what is happening in me, to express it concretely. So

I say. "Rabbi, I am a rich man, and today I promise to give one half of all that I have to the poor, and as for those I have cheated, I will repay them four times what I took."

Jesus continues gazing at me intently for a moment, but then his face relaxes and a smile lights it with joy. He raises his hand in a gesture of blessing, saying, "Today salvation has come to your house, Zacchaeus, because you too are a descendant of Abraham." Then, turning toward the crowd he adds, "For I have come to seek and save the lost."

What words! What a joy! I had forgotten that I am a son of Abraham. I have been so far from my people, my tradition, my God. Indeed, I have been lost, out of place, with no sense of belonging. But now Jesus is reaching out to me, calling to me. He is making it clear that he knows all about me and still accepts me. I have not done a thing to deserve his care, his interest, but he is choosing my house. He is treating me as one who belongs, a worthwhile human being.

This indeed is the meaning of salvation—
   *To know that I am accepted just as I am....
   *To realize I am not stuck in my dishonest way of
      life....I can grow and change.
   *To know to whom I belong and to act on that
      sense of belonging....
   *To live in new relationship with God and other
      people....

All this adds up to salvation—to health and wholeness.

As I look back on that great day, it is as if I had been traveling the same road, plodding along day after day, only to stop short and realize I am going in the wrong direction. Now, I know I must turn around and find a new road—one that leads toward the kind of goodness I see in Jesus.

The first step is to make amends for my cheating by paying people back and giving to those in need. I've been working on doing this for weeks now—ever since Jesus came to my house and we spent the afternoon together. I don't know what will come next. I am wondering if I can stay in my profession with my reputation. Will people ever trust me? Is it possible to be an honest tax collector? If I can continue, and function honestly, staying might ease the people's burden.

If I don't stay, I don't what I'll do. Maybe I'll make a complete change and leave Jericho. I am thinking of going to Jerusalem to find out what happened to Jesus. I heard that it was dangerous for him to go there. Many people were out to get him, to silence him and end his ministry. Maybe I could help—put up a ransom. Or even become one of his followers, like Matthew, the other tax collector.

Whatever happens, I know that I've changed for good. I know I'm on a new track, a new course. It may not be easy to stick to, but I believe that the memory of that commanding call to come down, and the power of the Holy Spirit will strengthen me and keep me moving in the right direction.

I doubt that you are like me. You haven't spent your life cheating and exploiting people. But you might have experienced a destructive pattern in your life, or felt your life was empty, at a stand still. Perhaps you've looked around and asked yourself, "Is that all there is?"

If you've ever felt this way, you may have searched for a new meaning, something to brighten and lighten your life. You may have sought out new friends or interests, a healthier life-style, studies, or other self-help. That's good, but I can tell you from my own experience that nothing, nothing can touch you and turn you and move you into newness of life like the love of God we meet in Jesus Christ. Nothing. And you don't have to go to the Jericho gate to find him. His living presence is in our midst, available to you, if only you will look, if only you will open yourself to it. Jesus is calling "Come down." He's waiting to go to your house today.

13

ONCE BLIND

(A Stewardship story sermon based on Mark 10:46-52)

INTRODUCTION

Stewardship is about building up the church and being God's generous hands in this aching world. Some Christians, both lay and clergy, don't like talking about money or stewardship. I worked with one lay leader who saw asking for pledges as a matter of begging. It's hard to understand that feeling if you love your church and want it to thrive. When you believe in something, you are enthusiastic. You want to support it and want other people to support it too. It also seems strange, when you remember that Jesus talked about money, possessions and our feelings and actions regarding them more than any other subject.

Stewardship involves vision. Learning to see in a fresh new way. That is the kind of sight that Bartimaeus gains along with his physical sight in today's Gospel lesson. It calls him into a new commitment as Jesus' disciple.

His story is the final healing narrative in Mark's Gospel and takes place toward the end, as Jesus and his disciples make their way to Jerusalem for the last time. After Bartimaeus tells his story, I will reflect on his experience in the hope that we too may open our eyes and follow Jesus on the way.

ONCE BLIND

The early spring sun is bathing my head and shoulders in warmth as I sit cross-legged here on the main street of Jericho. My cloth is spread out before me, ready to collect coins. Jericho is only about 15 miles from Jerusalem, on the main route to the holy city. The Passover festival is almost here and many pilgrims are on their way there to keep the feast. I can hear excited voices and feel the continual vibrations of many passing feet. Blind though I am, I can sense the crowd growing around me, bumping into me, jostling for position.

I'm hoping that all these pilgrims will mean money for me—that I can use their religious fervor to help my begging—maybe I will receive enough coins to eat for more than a day or two. I want them to see me, a blind beggar, and give generously as they travel to Jerusalem. After all, our God commands us to care about the needy. "Alms," I cry, "Pity a poor blind man."

"Be quiet," says a harsh voice. They're coming, and I want to hear to what the teacher is saying.

"What teacher? Who are you talking about? I have a right to beg."

"Haven't you heard," answers an impatient voice. "It is Jesus of Nazareth, the rebel rabbi who's been making a stir all over this land. Some say he is the Messiah, the Son of David. He and his followers are on their way to Jerusalem to celebrate Passover. Very soon now they'll pass us—I can see them just down the road.

Jesus of Nazareth, I stop and think. I have heard that name, and many stories about him. I have heard that he can heal the sick, that he even can make the lame walk and the blind see. Can it be true? I was not born blind, and tried every treatment I could find to heal my blindness until my money ran out. For years now I've pretty much given hope of seeing again, but it is still my dearest wish. As a blind man I'm isolated--cut off from people and so much of life. Maybe, just maybe, this Jesus can help me.

I picture Jesus coming nearer in my mind, walking as our teachers do, with a crowd of learners gathered around him, listening to his every word. The noise of the crowd is subsiding, and I hear a strong voice standing out above the others, speaking clearly and in thoughtful tones, explaining something.

I begin to cry, "Jesus, Son of David, have mercy on me!"

Then a man close to me calls out, "Silence! I'm trying to hear."

I do not obey his order. This is my only chance to be healed, my only chance to see again, to work again, to live again. I shout even louder, "Jesus, Son of David, have pity on me, help me."

More angry voices shush me, "Who do you think you are. Be quiet!"

But I keep on calling. "Son of David hear me." I can not let him pass me by. Oh if only I could see exactly where he is. If only I could run to him, kneel before him, entreat him to help me. More and more I feel sure that he truly has the power to heal.

Then I hear that strong, clear voice again, saying "Call the blind man to me." The teacher must have stopped near me.

Now the other voices stop scolding and encourage me. "Have courage." "Take heart." "Get up, Jesus is calling you"

Immediately, I throw off my cloak, spring to my feet and let the others lead me to Jesus. I feel him place his hand gently on my shoulder. He does not assume that he knows my desire, and I feel joy when he asks, "What do you want me to do for you?"

"My teacher, let me see again."

Jesus lays his hand firmly on my head and says "Go, your faith has made you well."

Immediately, I sense a new light streaming into my darkness. I blink, and open my eyes slowly. I partially shut them again against the brightness of the day, but then I open them wide. There is the road, the crowd, the bright blue day, the new leaves budding on the trees. Most of all, there is the teacher, smiling at me, looking at me with deep, dark compassionate eyes. I fall down before him to offer thanks, but he takes my hand and lifts to my feet.

"Master, I want to follow you."

He looks into my eyes, intently. Then he smiles again and nods, so I turn, pick up my cloak and join the other disciples, ready to follow Jesus. I once was blind, but now I can see the way.

* * * *

Blindness and sight, both physical and metaphorical, are major themes in scripture. People are struck blind, others are born that way. People like the Pharisees cannot see who Jesus is, while the poor do see, and hear him gladly. And people are healed of blindness. Scales fall from clouded eyes at a touch, new insights fill hearts. As the hymn, "Gather Us In," declares, when we come together before God, a new light is streaming—revealing truth, illuminating hearts, driving away doubt and calling us into service.

I love the story of Bartimaeus—the faith and energy and persistence which gain him healing and a new life of discipleship. The story is as much about Bartimaeus' call as it is of his healing. In fact he is healed of his blindness and gathered into discipleship all in one fell swoop.

Events happen fast, as they usually do in Mark's Gospel. The blind beggar reaches out for healing, and when Jesus calls him to come, he springs up immediately and responds. Jesus speaks and immediately

Bartimaeus regains his sight. And immediately his gratitude impels him follow Jesus on the way—which means following Jesus into Jerusalem, which means following him all the way to the cross. Bartimaeus is no fair weather disciple, and stands in contrast to the twelve, who seem so blind and dense during much of Mark's Gospel, and who have so much trouble understanding who Jesus is and what he must do. Bartimaeus sees clearly.

What does it take for Bartimaeus to be healed? First, He knows exactly what he wants and persists in the effort to get it. When he sees the possibility of healing he doesn't hesitate to call out for help. When people tell him to stop shouting, when they order him to be silent, he only yells louder. He will not stop trying, but insists on being heard.

Second, Bartimaeus believes. He believes that Jesus has the power to heal him. He trusts the stories he's heard and has faith that if he can only reach Jesus he will be healed. In fact it is his strong and steady faith that gives him the energy and determination to persist in shouting for Jesus' attention.

Like Bartimaeus, all through the years, people of faith have been healed from blindness and found new vision and new life through the power of our Lord. Think of how St. Paul is struck down and blinded on the road to Damascus, only to have his eyes opened to the living Christ and become the great apostle to the Gentiles.

Or remember how Martin Luther starts out as an obedient monk, blind to the abuses in the Roman Catholic Church of his day. Gradually his vision changes. He begins to see the error of teaching that believers can earn salvation. I love the story, perhaps apocryphal, of how Luther goes on a pilgrimage to Rome, and climbs the stairway up to Pontius Pilate's palace, the same staircase Jesus climbed the day he was condemned. The tradition was for pilgrims to climb the long staircase on their knees, reciting the Lord's Prayer on each step. They believed that each step they climbed while praying earned credits called indulgences which would shorten their time of purification in purgatory. The story says that Luther starts climbing the stairway, obediently reciting the prayer, only to spring to his feet halfway up crying, "The just shall live by faith." He had been blind to the folly of the tradition, but now he sees in a new way and goes on to lead the Protestant Reformation.

Think also of John Newton, who wrote the beloved hymn "Amazing Grace" back in the eighteenth century. He was captain of a slave ship, blind to the suffering of his human cargo. In March of 1848 he returned to England after a particularly stormy and terrifying trip from Africa, and began reading *The Imitation of Christ*, by the monk, Thomas A Kempis. The Holy Spirit used his frightening experience at sea and the inspirational thoughts he was reading to lead him into faith.

For awhile Newton continued as a slaver, holding worship services for his hardened crew and trying to improve conditions for the slaves. Soon he gave up trying to justify his work, and became a crusader against slavery. He studied for the ministry and started preaching the Gospel in the Anglican Church, where they affectionately called him "the old converted sea captain." He always stressed his personal salvation story and the simple heartfelt faith we hear in "Amazing Grace".

How about us? We too can be blind to God's call and action in our lives and communities, but if we open ourselves to God's seeking presence, we can know the fullness of life God holds out before us. We can see the blessings that shine upon us day by day.

You and I may not have had dramatic faith experiences like Bartimaeus, and these other giants of faith. But haven't there been times when you realize that you have been blind, or at least closed minded, on some idea or issue? Haven't you ever had the sense of your eyes being opened to new insights about life and the world and people? You hear a splendid speaker, see a program on TV, or read a book with a powerful fresh perspective and your vision begins to change, new thoughts emerge. It can be about something big—like war and peace, economic justice, energy or health care reform. You have an "A-ha" experience.

Or it can be something much smaller, much simpler. I sing in our little retirement community's chorus, and last Monday I fell before our rehearsal. I had been on my way to speak to someone and all of a sudden, there I was, flat on the floor, with no idea of how I got there and feeling utterly chagrined and embarrassed. Then I felt the director's strong hand clasping mine, lifting me back to my feet. A couple of other altos helped me to my chair, making sure I wasn't hurt. As I sat trying to catch my breath and collect myself, the singer behind me gave me a shoulder rub. After the rehearsal I was offered rides home and the next day a couple of people called to make sure there were no delayed repercussions from the fall. I have never been blind to the goodness of the people among whom I live, but tears came to my eyes as I experienced the level of their kindness and concern. I was so touched that I saw them anew, and will continue to see them with fresh eyes and appreciation.

Now I know that if you think about it, you can find the same sort of care and kindness right here in this church. When there is hurt or need, loneliness or sorrow the people step right up. And so as you move through this stewardship season, I call you to open your eyes to the light shining among you. Let it give you vision, and illuminate your caring for one another and this community. Let it re-awaken your sense of call and commitment. You are God's gathered people. Like Bartimaeus, may you see clearly and follow Jesus on the way.

14

LAVISH LOVE

(Based on John 12:1-7, Matthew 26:6-13,
Mark 14:3-9, Luke 10:38-42, I John 4:16-21)

INTRODUCTION

This story sermon begins with a story of lavish love and then reflects on how such love relates to our lives.

The story of a woman anointing Jesus before his passion appears in three of the four canonical Gospels, but only John identifies her as Mary of Bethany, the sister of Martha and Lazarus. Today, as Mary tells her story, I will be using John's version as a base, supplemented with verses from the other Gospels.

LAVISH LOVE

Jesus came to our house today. We live in Bethany, only two miles east of Jerusalem, so it is a good stopping point for him and his disciples as they journey to the holy city. It is only six days until Passover, and Jesus and his disciples want to celebrate the feast there.

I wouldn't be surprised if more than a celebration happens in Jerusalem this year. The religious authorities are growing angrier and angrier with Jesus. They hate the way he hob-nobs with prostitutes and tax collectors and all the other people they call sinners because they don't—or can't—obey all the rules of our religion. The tension is growing and I worry about violence erupting while he's there.

When we were together at the table today, I could sense that Jesus was feeling tension too. He must have been wondering about what might happen in Jerusalem. I thought back to happier days, when our friendship with Jesus began. All three of us, my brother Lazarus, my sister Martha and I had wonderful times with him. He cared about us all and had a unique relationship with each one of us. He treated Martha and me as if we were just as important as Lazarus—an unusual experience for women in our world. Jesus came and visited us as often as he could and always seemed to be able to find peace and relaxation in our home.

One time, we did have a little upset when Jesus was with us. We didn't know that he and his disciples were coming to see us until the last minute, and Martha was troubled about many things. What did we have in the house to eat? Did we have anything good enough for Jesus? And the house was a mess—we needed to clean up and get ready for this important company. Lazarus wasn't around, and I helped Martha at first, but when we heard the knock on the door I set down my broom and didn't pick it up again.

"Come on Martha, they're here," I called as I went to the door to greet Jesus and his friends. She joined me in welcoming them. They were so hot and tired from the dusty trip. We found them some water and a place to rest. Then I took Jesus apart, into a cool inner room and sat down quietly with him. Martha was still in the kitchen, but to me, it was more important to keep Jesus company than to produce a perfect meal.

We just sat for a while, with Jesus telling me stories from his ministry and sharing some of his concerns about the future. Then Martha came bustling in, with her hands on her hips and an aggrieved expression on her face. "There you are, Mary," she said. "I really need your help if we're going to feed all these guests." Then she spoke to

Jesus. "Lord, don't you care that my sister has left me to do all the work by myself? Tell her to help me."

Immediately, Jesus spoke up and said gently, "Martha, Martha, you are worried and distracted by many things; there is need for only one thing. Mary has chosen the better part, which will not be taken away from her."

I could hardly believe my ears. Instead of rebuking me and relegating me to the usual woman's place in the kitchen, Jesus was affirming my desire to be a disciple, a learner. All my life I have been judged lacking because I am too interested in male activities, like listening and learning and discussing thoughts and ideas. Women aren't supposed to be interested or involved in such things. Now here was my dear teacher saying it was fine for me—in fact he called it the "better part."

Of course Jesus' words didn't make Martha happy, but I think it helped that even as he spoke, he stood and started toward the kitchen to give her a hand. Of course I did too. Martha has always been the practical one, the person who takes care of life's details, but that doesn't mean that she doesn't think deep thoughts too, and Jesus knows it.

That visit was a fine experience for me, and I think it was one of the reasons that I dared to do what I did when Jesus came today. This time he looked even more tired and drained than the last, and I wanted to do something that might relax and soothe him. Lazarus was reclining with Jesus and the others at the table, and Martha was serving, as usual. I had been helping her, but I put down my serving dish, and went to my room where I had been keeping a treasured jar of costly nard, a whole pound of perfumed ointment. I brought it back to the table and knelt down at Jesus' feet. Gently, I picked up one foot and began massaging in the fragrant ointment. Then I took and massaged the other foot, hoping that my touch and the ointment would heal the soreness and ease both his body and soul.

Jesus was leaning back, releasing the tension that held him and I was concentrating on rubbing in the nard and wiping Jesus' feet with my hair, when an angry voice interrupted me. "What do you think you're doing, woman?" It was Judas Iscariot, one of the disciples. "Why are you wasting that perfume? Why didn't you sell it for 300 denarii and give the money to the poor?" I doubted that he was that concerned about the poor, but I knew Judas cared a lot about being in charge of the disciples' money.

I sat up straight, ready to answer him, but Jesus spoke first. He said "Leave her alone. Mary has anointed me beforehand for my burial. You always have the poor with you and can help them anytime, but you do not always have me." Then he added these amazing words, "Truly I tell you, wherever the good news is proclaimed in the whole world, what she has done will be told in remembrance of her." Would I really be remembered for anointing Jesus?

What mattered most to me was that when I brought out the fragrant nard it did not offend Jesus. He understood that I did not intend to neglect the poor, but wanted to give him the very best gift I had. I wanted to give as generously, extravagantly and lavishly as he had given to me. And he received my gift as it was intended, with appreciation, pleasure and joy.

It felt good to hear Jesus defending me, but at the same time I felt a strange chill moving through my body. Why did he speak of his burial? Perhaps my fears of what might happen in Jerusalem were well founded. Clearly, Jesus was expecting to die soon. Now I felt even better about choosing not to hold back, but rather to give my most lavish gift to express my love and thanks to my Lord. Praise be to God!

* * * * *

Lavish love. Giving unstintingly without thought of holding anything back. This is the kind of love Mary showered on Jesus that day in Bethany. This is the kind of love Jesus lived and gave, finally offering his very life for his friends, for us. This lavish love resembles nothing less than the love of God--*agape*, self giving love.

Many people give the least they can to others, the lesser value, what they must. Instead of reaching out with hands open to offer the best they have, their hands stay clenched into tight fists, and their hearts hold back in self-protection. This story of Mary calls us out of that stingy sort of love, which can scarcely be called love, into the lavish love Jesus offered and she emulated.

I'm sure you know people who give this kind of lavish love. There are many in this church, and perhaps you are one of them yourself. When I think of the people I know who do this, I think first and foremost of my husband, Walter. Generosity and lavish love characterized the way he lived and loved.

Every April, when I honor the anniversary of Walter's death, I remember how much he enjoyed the springtime and early summer—from the first blossoming of the flowering trees, to the bursting forth of his beloved roses, he delighted in nature's lavish generosity. Early every spring we used to drive an elderly friend—even more elderly than we--over to the Ironstone Winery in the town of Murphys to see their lavish display of daffodils massed along the road and to exclaim over all the barrels filled with exotic daffodil varieties, hyacinths and tulips. It is an amazing and lovely sight—a great gift to the community—and every year they plant more and more bulbs—never saying, "That's enough."

Generosity, lavishness--is the philosophy Walter appreciated. He liked to say "If some is good, more is better." Sometimes following this idea got him into trouble. He was a devoted gardener who usually produced magnificent results with his labors. But one year, as his faculties were diminishing, he decided to be extra lavish with fish fertilizer. Have you ever used it? When he finished feeding the plants in our patio garden everything smelled to high heaven and we had to keep the door to the house tight closed. An onslaught of flies swarmed in the flower bed and we needed professional help to get rid of them. One liquid amber tree was also the recipient of this generous feeding and almost died, but after several years it has finally recovered.

The "if some is good more is better" philosophy doesn't work with fertilizer, but when it comes to passing out love it usually does. Walter did this constantly as well. If we were exploring a town looking at the shop windows—he was one of those rare men who enjoys window shopping-- I had to protect our budget by being careful of what I admired, because surely he would suggest going in and buying the item for me whether we could afford it or not. And of course this giving spirit wasn't confined to things, but included expressions of affection, offering comfort, courage and whatever help was needed. He gave lavishly to me, the rest of the family, friends, parishioners, and causes he believed in —reaching out and doing as much as he possibly could.

Lavish love, generous giving, characterize the nature and love of God. God created this world and us and all the other creatures who live in within it, out of the pure desire to give. Even though we often hoard, squander and spoil them, God filled the earth with the resources we need for life, and continues to supply our needs, calling us to love and share lavishly as well—especially with those who do not have enough.

How do we learn to love lavishly? I believe that ability is a gift of God—as I John says, "We love because God first loved us."(I John 4:16-21) At the same time, lavish love can be developed by cultivating a spirit of gratitude and appreciation. Walter was a person who spent a lot of time counting his blessings instead of his troubles, and was filled with gratitude for the love he had received and was receiving in life.

Walter grew up in Memphis, Tennessee. His family was poor, though as he often said, they never went hungry. His parents were loving, but strict, and he worked in his father's hardware store from the time he was six years old. They offered him the gift of faith, taking him to the Methodist church to learn and worship regularly. There he made friends in the youth group and had a lot of fun as well. From this humble childhood, Walter went on to attend to Duke University, a Methodist institution, which gave him a full scholarship because he was planning to become a minister. He was able to work to pay for his room and board, and never stopped being thankful for the great opportunity of his education. He felt the same way about attending seminary, going to China as a missionary, and all the churches he served. Each call was a treasured gift, and when he retired he gladly continued assisting in the churches I served and we attended.

As he grew older, Walter undertook an active ministry of prayer. He vision was failing and he could no longer read, so he spent hours praying, lying down or sitting quietly in his chair. He offered constant prayer for people with special needs and for the whole world, letting God and all of us know his concerns. Daily, he gave thanks for his family, education, pastorates, parishioners, friends and me. Most of all, he was grateful to God, believing that he had been given much and forgiven much all through his life. He embodied lavish love received and given.

Walter believed that lavish love flows out of gratitude, and so do I. He often said that gratitude is one of the highest virtues and ingratitude, one of the worst sins. It's all too easy to lack appreciation if we believe that we're entitled to everything we are and everything we have. Instead of believing we are blessed, we think we just have what we deserve. We forget the reality of amazing grace, the undeserved, lavish love we receive from God and other people. But if we count the blessings of our lives daily—and even in times of trouble we can find something to be thankful for—we will find a spirit of gratitude begin to bubble up within us. The more we feel it, the more it will grow into an abundant river issuing into the desire to love lavishly and give as we have received. Try it, dear friends, just try it. Find the joy of receiving and giving lavish love.

15

I HAVE SEEN THE LORD

(Luke 8:1-3, John 20:1-18)

INTRODUCTION

Mary Magdalene has always been a figure of great interest among church people. Way back in 591 A.D., Pope Gregory I planted the seed of the persistent belief that she was a prostitute by identifying her with the un-named sinful woman in the seventh chapter of Luke's gospel. There is no scriptural evidence for saying the two women are the same.

Mary was a dear friend and disciple of Jesus, and in our time, some popular novelists have presented her as Jesus' lover or wife. For example, in *The Da Vince Code*, Dan Brown postulates that Mary and Jesus were married and started a family.

All this is interesting and intriguing, but not particularly helpful for faith and life. In contrast, I find it both thought provoking and meaningful to think about the way a twelfth century monk named Bernard of Clairvaux, spoke of Mary Magdalene. He called her the "apostle to the apostles," because she was the first to carry the news of seeing the risen Christ to the disciples huddled together in Jerusalem. (John 20:18) Nowadays, Biblical scholars are focusing on this and recovering Mary's centrality as the first witness to the resurrection of Jesus Christ.

You probably know that the four gospels are not written as biographies of Jesus. There are differences between them, but they share the same purpose. They all proclaim the good news of God's love bursting into the world in Jesus Christ, but each does this is its own way within its own narrative world.

In John's gospel, for example, Mary Magdalene does not appear until the passion story. We first meet her standing at the foot of the cross with the "beloved disciple" and three other women. Unlike the women in the first three gospels, she is not looking on at the crucifixion from afar. The only other time she appears in the gospel of John is on Easter morning when she goes to visit Jesus' tomb.

Today's story/sermon will be grounded primarily in John's narrative world, drawing only briefly on the other gospels for background material about Mary's relationship to Jesus and the rest of the disciples. This means that you may notice some differences from the other gospel accounts—for example, Mary does not go to the tomb in order to prepare Jesus' body for burial, and she goes, not with the other women, but alone.

Now hear the story of Easter morning as told by the Gospel of John in chapter 20:1-18.

I HAVE SEEN THE LORD

It was still dark when I slipped out of the small room where I was staying in Jerusalem. Oh, I knew it was unheard of for a woman to go out alone at that hour but I had no choice. Now that the Sabbath was finally over I had to go and mourn at the garden tomb. I had to see where they had laid Jesus to rest.

The events of these last days seemed unreal, like walking through a dream. Maybe you've felt that way when you've lost a loved one. You can't seem to take it in, absorb it. You expect to see that beloved face, to hear that familiar voice.....That's the way it was for me, Mary of Magdala. I had to go to the garden and see the tomb sealed with a huge round stone. Then perhaps I could believe that Jesus was really dead.

The years of working with him were never easy but always good! Let me tell you the story as I lived it.

My life began in Magdala, a big city and important trading center on the west shore of the Sea of Galilee. It bustled with activity—boat building, fishing, fish curing and agriculture. You name it, and it was happening in Magdala.

But not all the activity was constructive. Magdala was known as a wicked city, notorious for every kind of corruption and vice. It was a lot like Babylon, that ancient center of sinful and dissolute living.

Economically, Magdala had extremes of wealth and poverty. My family was prosperous, so I was fortunate enough to live well removed from the sordid side of the city's life. I never suffered the kind of poverty and despair that led so many of its women into lives of prostitution.

Does that surprise you? You always thought that I was a scarlet woman, a whore? Well, that painful rumor's been around a long time. I know what people say, even though there's not a word in scripture to support it.

I don't know how the rumor started. Maybe it was because of my home city's reputation, or because I was unconventional enough to travel with Jesus and the twelve. A lot of folks though that only a loose woman would go off heaven knows where with a group of men.

I hate to think it, but the gossip could have come from the other disciples. Sometimes they, especially Peter, seemed jealous of my friendship with Jesus. I remember the time he accused me of dominating the conversation with Jesus, and trying to displace him and the other disciples. (Elaine Pagels reports this and other instances of tension between Mary and Peter in *The Gnostic Gospels*, Vintage Books, NY, 1979, pp. 77-79.)

Or again, the stories could have begun because of my strange and terrible illness. Many people think that if a woman has a mysterious disorder or ailment it must have to do with sex. If you say "woman" and "sinner" in the same breath they don't think of greed or pride or dishonesty, but assume the sin is sexual.

Actually, no one has ever figured out exactly what was wrong with me. From childhood I had been ill—mentally, physically and emotionally. The symptoms were frightening! I had seizures, couldn't recognize people and sometimes lost my sight and hearing. Sometimes I said and did things I couldn't remember.

I felt as though I had too many selves, or no self, or that I had lost myself. You might call my illness schizophrenia now, but in my time we didn't know such names. We just said I was possessed by demons—evil spirits.

My parents searched high and low for healing for me. We saw many physicians and tried innumerable cures, but nothing helped. Nothing, that is, until I met Jesus, my Savior and my Lord.

I don't know how he healed me—they say he drove not one, but seven, demons out of me. Maybe it was a word, a touch, or just his powerful presence that did it, but I know that last I felt whole. I was one person, not many at war with one another.

Being near Jesus continued to heal me and I grew strong enough to help in his ministry. Jesus and the twelve accepted me as a friend and co-worker. I joined with them and a few other women who dared to follow Jesus.

My father had set up an endowment for me, thinking that I would always need special care. Now I was well and could use it for the One who had healed me and given me back my life. It gave me joy to be able to contribute money for food and other necessities for our little band.

What an amazing time we had working and traveling as Jesus taught and preached and healed! I loved listening to his stories and watching the way he worked with people. He accepted the folks everyone else rejected. It wouldn't have mattered to him if I had been a prostitute. He knew what life was like for women—how few choices we had, especially if we were poor or alone.

Jesus got into trouble with the religious authorities for welcoming everyone who turned to him, and even sitting down to eat with prostitutes and sinners—unheard of for a rabbi. He refused to worry about the familiar labels, "clean" and "unclean." In fact, he taught us that only what comes out of you can make you unclean, not anything you eat or anyone you touch.(Matt. 15:1—20)

In those days together, we shared laughter and storytelling, but also hard journeys and disagreements. Even though Jesus kept saying his kingdom was not of this world, that he was a different kind of Messiah, a lot of us felt sure he would end up operating as the political leader we'd always expected. We wanted him to deliver us from the power of Rome.

When we turned toward Jerusalem for Passover that last time, we sensed that the climax of Jesus' ministry would come during the holy season. He even said, "The hour is come for the Son of Man to be glorified."(John 12:23) But we had no idea what he meant or how horrible the way to his glorification would be.

The other women and I stayed in the Upper Room after our last Passover meal, while Jesus and the men went out to the Garden of Gethsemane. We did not see Judas with the band of soldiers, the betrayal or the arrest. How terrifying it must have been! No wonder the men ran and hid. No wonder Peter denied even knowing him.

As women, we ran less risk of arrest, but even for us it was dangerous to be associated with Jesus. Still, we determined to go and see what was happening. So the next day, when they led him out to be crucified, we followed all the way to the cross. We saw the inscription—"Jesus of Nazareth, King of the Jews"—and we watched the soldiers casting lots for his clothing.

His mother, Mary, and her sister, and Mary, the wife of Clopas, stayed with me at the base of the cross. By then John, the beloved disciple, had dared to return, and he stood beside us.

How hard it is to remember, let alone speak of that scene—the mocking words, flies buzzing, blood, thirst, excruciating pain. We saw it all. But we also heard Jesus shout those triumphant words—"It is finished."(John 19:30) He had completed the work God had given him to do.

We watched as they took down that poor, broken body, and as Joseph of Arimathea arranged to have him buried in a new tomb in a garden nearby. We followed along to the tomb and saw Nicodemus arrive with myrrh and aloe to prepare the body. They used spices and linen cloths to wrap him quickly, as the Sabbath was near, when everyone would have to stop working and rest.

Rest! How could we rest again after all this? We were scattered and demoralized, within and without. How could we rest when the One who was the center of our lives was gone? How could we rest?

After tossing and turning all that night and fretting through the Sabbath, only to lie awake again, I decided I must go to the tomb. If I saw it in all its finality, perhaps I could accept Jesus' death as reality.

So as I told you, I slipped out before first light and hurried to the tomb. When I arrived, I peered into the gloom. By then it was light enough to make out the tomb's entrance and I could see that the stone sealing the doorway had been rolled away. The tomb was standing wide open!

Later, I remembered how Jesus had spoken of being raised from the dead, but at that moment, I could only think, "Grave robbers. Someone has stolen his body, taken him away."

I turned and ran back to the place where the disciples were hiding and found Peter and the disciple Jesus loved. They both came running and it was a regular footrace! I was so tired from running to get them that they soon left me trailing behind. By the time I got to the tomb they already had looked inside and were heading back to town.

Peter looked bewildered, but the other disciple had an exalted expression on his face. What could it mean? My tears began to flow. It was just too much. I decided to stay in the garden awhile, sorting things out.

By now there was more light, so I bent down to look inside that cave-like tomb again. I could see the ledge carved out of the rock wall, where they had laid Jesus' body. The grave cloths were still there, but now I saw two angels, one where Jesus' head had been, and the other, at the foot.

They asked me why I was weeping. "Because they've taken away my Lord and I don't know where they've laid him." Surely it was the final indignity that he had not been left to rest in peace.

I turned away from the tomb, and saw someone—maybe the gardener—someone in charge who might have some answers. Before I could speak, he asked me, "Woman, why are you weeping? Whom do you seek?

"O please sir, if you have carried him away, tell me where you have laid him and I will take him."

Then he said my name in Hebrew, "Miriam." That voice—that voice—instantly I knew it was Jesus. Only he called my name that way.

"Rabboni!" I cried. "My dear teacher!" I sprang forward to throw my arms around him.

But he drew back, saying "Do not cling to me."

At first I felt hurt, but then I realized that even though this was the same Jesus who had been crucified, he was not the same. God had transformed him into a new creation. I had to let go of our old relationship in order to enter the new, permanent one he had promised. I had to release Jesus if I was going to embrace the Risen Christ. I could not cling to him, lean on him, any more. In fact he was counting on me, calling me into responsibility and action.

He said, "Go to my brothers, and say I am ascending to my Father and your Father, to my God and your God." Christ was commissioning me to be the first witness to his Resurrection. Imagine, he was choosing me, a woman, to be apostle to the apostles.

I ran back to the city and burst into the room where the disciples were gathered, exclaiming, "I have seen the Lord!"

Yes, I have seen the Lord. I know from my own experience that he is alive. Do you believe that? Can you believe me and the other witnesses even though you weren't there to see for yourself? Do you remember how he said to Thomas, "Blessed are those who do not see and yet believe? (John 20:29) If it is difficult for you to believe, think for a moment about the events that happened after that amazing morning. We, his followers, came together as never before. The Holy Spirit gathered our bedraggled, uncertain band of disciples and mobilized us into a powerful, courageous team of apostles. We went out into the whole world we knew to proclaim the good news that Christ is alive.

Jesus' resurrection changed us and the world forever. In Christ, God had let loose a new power for loving and serving. Other lives changed too. Followers of the crucified and risen Savior have created schools, churches and hospitals. They are still doing works of caring and struggling for justice and mercy in his name.

Beloved friends, the life changing power of the Risen Christ can fill you too. Try opening your heart and mind and soul to him and let his presence confront you.

And make no mistake, a confrontation with him is as decisive as having your new baby placed in your arms. Remember or imagine that moment. This child is your child to cherish, nurture and guide. When you look down into that little face you are confronted with a life that is going to change you and your life forever—a life that will require you to grow as never before.

Being confronted with the reality of the Risen Christ is not that different. If you open yourself to him and allow his Spirit and quality of life to penetrate your being, you will change and grow. You will challenge your values and re-order your priorities. Along with the family of Christ we call the church you will learn to reach out to others, doing and telling the good news of God's love.

Today I have called you to join me inside the Gospel story, to feel the goodness of working with Jesus, the terror of seeing his death, the joy of experiencing his risen presence and the exhilaration of hearing and obeying his commission to "go and tell" the good news.

You may not see the Lord face to face, but you can know his presence and power right here, right now. May it be so.

16

FIFTY DAYS AFTER

(Luke 8:1-3, Acts 2:1-47)

This morning I invite you to take a trip in your imagination—back to first century Jerusalem on the day of the first Pentecost after Jesus' resurrection.

My name is Joanna. I am one of the women doctor Luke writes about in chapter eight of his Gospel, one of several women who work and travel and minister with Jesus and his other disciples. (Luke 8:1-3)

I live a strange life with Jesus—strange and shocking for my time. It just isn't done for a woman to travel with a group of men. Still it might have seemed strange for anyone. Following Jesus means having no real home. As he put it, "Foxes have holes and birds have nests, but the Son of Man has no place to lay his head"(Luke 9:58)—and neither do we. Being with Jesus means getting up and going at a moment's notice, leaving everything behind, and associating with outcasts and undesirables. We have no security in the usual sense, and yet we feel the deepest kind of security when we are with him.

My life as a disciple is strange and demanding, but good. We feel that we are using our lives as they are meant to be used. But the highest point of all doesn't come until the day of Pentecost. By then we have lived through the trauma of Jesus' terrible death and the feeling that everything was over, ended. But our dull depression gives way to the trembling joy of Easter, when our spirits revive, knowing that he lives again. We have the reassurance of seeing him not once, but several times.

Then comes another shock. Jesus tells us he must leave us to be with God. What are we to do without him? He promises that we will not be alone, the Holy Spirit will come to strengthen and guide us.

But we are still afraid—like little children whose mother goes out and says, "Don't worry, I'll be right back." We know and trust Jesus, but still feel shaky, unsure of ourselves.

"Right back" seems like a dreadfully long time to us. Counting from Passover and Easter, we have been waiting more than a month. In fact it is fifty days, almost two months. It seems like forever! Will the Spirit really come? And when?

Every day we meet together to keep up our courage—the eleven, and later Matthew who takes the place of Judas; Jesus' mother, Mary, and his brothers; the rest of the women and me. We do our best to practice patience, after all we do have each other. We try to conquer our fear and anxiety, but we need more than each other. We need Jesus, our Lord.

Then the fiftieth day dawns. Try to picture the scene. It is the great festival of Pentecost, and what a day it is! Our people love this holiday, with its celebrations and freedom from work. It is one of our three great holidays, when all good Jews are expected to come to the holy city. Travel conditions are at their best in springtime, and religious Jews from every country under heaven gather in Jerusalem and fill the streets.

On Pentecost everyone celebrates two of God's great gifts. One is the first fruits of the harvest. The barley harvest is newly gathered, so we rejoice in that and offer God the first two loaves of barley bread. We also celebrate God's gift of the law to Moses on Mt. Sinai—that precious law which unifies us as a people and teaches us how to live together. It is a holiday overflowing with meaning.

We who love and follow Jesus are celebrating with everyone else, but we are waiting for another gift—the gift of the Holy Spirit. That morning we are gathered again in an upper room, removing ourselves from the crowds for awhile. At first everything goes as usual. We talk and pray. But then, what excitement! First we hear a great sound, like the rush of a mighty wind. All my life I'd heard of Elijah, and how God spoke to him in a still, small voice, but this is nothing like that. This wind, the Breath of God, literally roars as it swoops and swirls among us. It seems to breathe new life into us, just as it did into the first human beings when God created the world.

That wild wind is amazing enough, but the Spirit isn't finished with us yet. Suddenly, tongues of fire start licking and leaping around us. It is terrifying, especially when the flames actually touch us. But they don't hurt, and don't even singe us. It reminds me of the story of that burning bush Moses saw when God called him—the one that burned and burned without burning up.(Exodus 3:3—6)

On that Pentecost morning the Spirit came to us in wind and fire, but even they are not enough. Soon comes the most dramatic moment of all. We begin speaking all at once, but we speak, not in our own language, but in other tongues. Everyone speaks differently, yet somehow we can understand each other and communicate. Miraculous!

Well, we must be making a quite a racket, because the people outside on the street hear us through the open windows. They begin gathering around, looking up with surprised and puzzled faces. Here they are from many lands, and yet they are listening to these different languages and hearing not confusion, but their own tongues, telling the mighty acts of God.

They don't know what to make of it, and questions start flying thick and fast. "What's going on up there?" "What does this mean?

Some people think they are witnessing a miracle, but others mutter in disgust, "They must be drunk."

All I know is that I'm not drunk, but my speech is not my own. It is coming through me, not from me. Somehow I know I am speaking Libyan, though I've never heard it before. Next to me, Andrew is rattling on in Mesopotamian and Peter is speaking Greek with the ease of a native. All these languages, and yet we can understand each other.

I keep thinking of the old story of the tower of Babel. Do you remember how those ancient people try to unite and make a name for themselves by building a tower to the heavens? God responds by giving them all different languages so they can't understand each other and act so arrogantly again.(Genesis 11:1-9) Well, this Pentecost experience is like the reversal of Babel. Here we are, chattering in different languages, but instead of being confused, we understand each other with perfect clarity. It is as if God's Spirit is breaking through Babel, all our human divisions, and creating a new unity with room for everyone. Today, the Spirit is creating the unity those Babel builders could never build for themselves.

On that first Pentecost morning, we experienced a wonderful unity in the Spirit. You can still experience that unity, no matter what language you speak, no matter what country you call home. The good news of the Gospel is for everyone!

But I'm getting away from my story. As the wind and fire subside, and our speaking ends, questions keep coming from the crowd. Peter, good old Peter, stands up to respond. I can tell he feels insulted by comments about our being drunk—after all it is only nine o'clock in the morning—but most of all, he wants everyone to know the truth of what is happening.

What a magnificent speech he makes! I never dreamed Peter could speak like that. Now you would call it a sermon, and perhaps it is the first sermon. We listen carefully as he reviews our faith story: how God plans to heal the fallen world through Jesus Christ and how the Hebrew prophets foretold everything that has happened; how Jesus was put to death by our people and the Romans, and how God raised and exalted him. Now, Peter proclaims, the Spirit is being poured out on us, God's sons and daughters.

Many people are moved by Peter's passionate words. It hurts them to think that they have had a part in crucifying Jesus. They turn to each other and to Peter, asking, "What then, shall we do?"

Peter answers clearly, and without hesitation: First, repent, turn your life around. Move away from your old ways and toward God. Second, be baptized. Receive forgiveness and enter into the family of Christ. Third, receive the Holy Spirit. Wait for the power we are experiencing, the gift of the Spirit that will guide your life always

REPENT, BE BAPTIZED, RECEIVE THE HOLY SPIRIT. Peter knows it isn't enough to listen and hear, or even to feel and believe. If people truly believe, they have to act, to commit themselves to a new kind of life. Many say yes to Peter's invitation and 3000 are baptized that very day. Since then, more and more are entering our community of disciples, and we are meeting constantly. (Church meetings are nothing new you know!) We pray and plan and teach. We share our lives and break bread together. It is a fellowship like none we've ever known before.

Nowadays, you still remember and celebrate that first Pentecost and all the amazing things that happened. You use red altar cloths symbolizing the flames of fire. You sing Spirit hymns and read the story in the book of Acts.

Often you call Pentecost the birthday of the Church, because a brand new community was born that day, a community where everyone can be different and yet together in faith, a community strong enough to go out and witness in the world.

Pentecost is a birthday, all right, not only for the church, but for me and every person gathered in that room. It gives us a new start, a new meaning, a new purpose and power.

How about you? Have you had that kind of a birthday? Have you felt the Spirit moving and alive in your life? It doesn't have to be dramatic, with roaring wind and flames of fire—but you'll know when it happens, because you'll feel the Presence of the Spirit. Can you imagine that? The Breath of God blowing in and through your life—changing, cleansing, clarifying? Can you imagine, or have you felt the warmth of the Sprit's fire glowing in your heart? Has a tongue of holy flame rested on you, even for a moment, sparking your enthusiasm, inflaming your will?

Do you believe such a thing is possible, even now, in this cynical and scientific age of ours? Do you believe that the Holy Spirit is still active in you, and in your life together here in this church?

Dear friends, it is not enough to think of Pentecost as a day long past, to be remembered with wonder and celebrated once a year. That day of the Spirit is meant to flood your life with energy and purpose every day, as you work and worship together in your community of faith.

Our generation, the first generation of the church, is gone now, along with many others. In these days it is you, among others, who are the church of Jesus Christ. And it doesn't matter if your congregation is large or small. What matters is your willingness to open yourselves to the touch of the Spirit so the Holy Breeze can blow you in the right direction and the Holy Fire can kindle your heart and will.

It was not, and is not, easy to be the church. The challenges both within and out in the world are enormous. How can you be true to your faith while coping in this skeptical world? How can you manage serious differences of opinion and conviction among yourselves and communicate, just as we did? You do not have to be like Babel. With the help and power of the Holy Spirit you can be, and become, a faithful community, effective in your ministry and one in the Lord. May it be so.

EPILOGUE

THE STORY GOES ON…..

These voices from The Story have fallen silent. They have told their stories in the longing to be heard and understood, and hope that they have spoken to your heart.

These and all the other biblical voices are not the end of The Story. It has been going on for generations and continues now as God works to save through the weakness and power, inadequacy and grandeur, faithlessness and dedication of believers and the community called church. Individually and together we can add our voices to theirs and tell our stories.

The promise is that God's salvation story does not end with this life. Believers trust that in Christ they will live eternally with God. And more, they trust that God will bring history as we know it to an end and fashion a brand new creation. On that day, God will make all things new, and wipe away all the tears. Yes, all the tears! (Revelation 21:1-5)

Even so come, Lord Jesus.

BIBLIOGRAPHY

The primary source for this book is <u>The Holy Bible</u>. The quotations are primarily from the New Revised Standard Version, but I have consulted various translations and paraphrases.

OTHER WORKS CONSULTED

Anderson, Bernhard W. <u>The Unfolding Drama of the Bible,</u> New York: Association Press, 1971

Barclay, William. <u>The Daily Study Bible</u>, Edinburgh, Scotland: Saint Andrew Press, 1958 Commentaries on Matthew, Mark, Luke, John and Acts

Breech, James. <u>The Silence of Jesus</u>, Canada: Doubleday, 1983

Brown, Raymond E., The Birth of the Messiah, Garden City, NY, Doubleday & Co. Inc., 1977

Brueggemann, Walter. <u>Genesis</u>, an Interpretation Commentary, Atlanta, Georgia: John Knox Press, 1982

_____. <u>I Kings</u>, Knox Preaching Guides, Atlanta, Georgia: John Knox Press, 1982

_____. <u>First and Second Samuel</u>, an Interpretation Commentary, Louisville, Kentucky: John Knox Press, 1990

Buechner, Frederick. <u>Peculiar Treasures</u>, New York: Harper and Row, and Toronto, Fitzhenry and Whiteside Limited, 1979

Emswiler, Sharon Neufer. The Ongoing Journey: Women and the Bible, np: Board of Global Ministries, The United Methodist Church, 1977

Fiorenza, Elisabeth Schussler. In Memory of Her, New York: The Crossroad Publishing Co., 1983

Grassi, Carolyn M. and Joseph A. Mary Magdalene and the Women in Jesus' Life, Kansas City, Missouri: Sheed and Ward, 1986

Hertzberg, Hans Wilhelm Hertzberg. I & II Samuel, Philadelphia, Pennsylvania: The Westminster Press, 1976

Trible, Phyllis. Texts of Terror, Philadelphia, Pennsylvania: The Fortress Press, 1984

Wahlberg, Rachel Conrad. Jesus According to a Woman, Mahwah, New Jersey: Paulist Press, 1975

_____. Jesus and the Freed Woman, New York: The Paulist Press, 1978

Wiesel, Elie. Messengers of God, New York: Random House, 1977

_____. Sages and Dreamers, New York: Summit Books, Simon and Schuster Inc., 1991